FREELANCING BY DESIGN

Essential strategies and proven tactics to build a thriving freelance business from your creative work

ALVALYN LUNDGREN

Alvalyn creative

Published by Alvalyn Lundgren | Alvalyn Creative LLC
Thousand Oaks, CA 91320 USA
https://alvalyncreative.com
https://alvalyn.com
https://freelanceroadtrip.com

Printed in the United States of America

ISBN 979-8-9953004-0-3

Cover design and interior pages design by Alvalyn Lundgren.

Typography: Avenir Next Condensed, Thirsty Rough, Questa

Alvalyn creative

LEGAL DISCLAIMER: The contents of this book are provided as information and education only, and are not intended to be taken as legal, tax, or professional advice. The author's intent is to provide general business education and information only and not as a substitute for professional legal or financial advice. Any included legal and tax information is intended to be general in nature and not necessarily to reflect current laws at the time of your reading. Laws and regulations vary based on jurisdiction, and change frequently. The reader should not construe any information as legal advice specific to their situation, but should consult with a legal or tax professional for counsel specific to their circumstances. Reliance on any information contained in this book is solely at the reader's own risk. The author and Alvalyn Creative disclaim any and all liability in connection with actions taken or not taken based on the content of this book. Use of this book does not create an attorney-client, accountant-client, or any other professional relationship between the reader and the author or Alvalyn Creative. By using this book you acknowledge and agree to the above terms and understand that neither the author or Alvalyn Creative is responsible for any legal, tax, or professional decisions made by the reader based on the information included.

DISCLOSURE: While the author utilized artificial intelligence (AI) along with internet sources as part of her research for this book, AI was not utilized to write. It's all human-created.

This book is dedicated to my daughter, Sarah Tirzah,
who, like me, is a freelance creative.

... and he has filled him with the Spirit of God, with skill,
with intelligence, with knowledge, and with all craftsmanship,
to devise artistic designs, to work in gold and silver and bronze,
in cutting stones for setting, and in carving wood, for work
in every skilled craft.

EXODUS 35:31–33 ESV

... and to aspire to live quietly, and to mind your own affairs,
and to work with your hands, as we instructed you ...

I THESSALONIANS 4:11 ESV

"Calling ten of his servants, he gave them ten minas,
and said to them, 'Engage in business until I come.' "

LUKE 19:13 ESV

CONTENTS

INTRODUCTION

THEY DON'T TEACH THIS IN DESIGN SCHOOL.

If you went to school and developed a creative portfolio, you now have a body of work and, if you're like I was, you're clueless about how to earn a living from it aside from working for someone else. But what if you're entrepreneurial? How do you leverage your creative skills to transform yourself into a successful creative entrepreneur — a *creativepreneur*?

If you didn't go to school but want to earn a living as a freelance creative, how do you go about it? What do you need to know? What steps should you take? It's not creative skills alone. You need to add business skills.

There's a gap between your creative skills and what you must know in order to build a thriving creative business. Design school does not teach you how to market yourself, how to work with clients, or how to build your brand. And it certainly doesn't teach you how to build a business. What art school is good for and excels in is developing that portfolio. How do you bridge that gap and blend these seemingly unrelated pursuits — creativity and business — into a thriving career? How do you do this if your ideal future is all about building your own business as a freelancer?

If you're self-taught, you've probably focused on learning software, typography, color, grid systems, drawing, and design principles. Your focus is on technique, generally. You've pursued and done well with the creative work, but how do you earn a living from it as an independent contractor?

A BURGEONING FREELANCE ECONOMY

According a 2025 study by Upwork Research Institute*, 28% of all US-based skilled knowledge workers are working independently, comprising a $1.5 trillion industry. The traditional 9–5 work model is waning as people, especially creatives, pursue flexibility, financial control, and opportunity for innovation and significant work.

Art and design certificate and degree programs don't prepare creatives to freelance. Instead, they focus on grooming students to be hired by creative firms. Employer hiring rates are measurable and help schools market their programs, while the entrepreneurs among us don't get counted.

While employment and the sense of job security that comes with it is what most people aspire to, not every creative dreams of being an employee helping to build someone else's enterprise. An increasing percentage desire to launch their own businesses, and a large proportion want to freelance and serve clients instead of or in addition to selling products. There's a gap that divides creativity from business that's not addressed in business or design school, and not sufficiently within the creative professions, either.

DEFINING THE GAP

Suppose you've been freelancing for a few years. You've acquired a decent amount of clients and are able to remain independent. But you find yourself dealing with recurring problems. One client doesn't pay. Another keeps piling on work. Another demands discounts and special treatment. Another tells you how you should do your job. Another treats you as their personal assistant and asks you to feed their dog and water their plants while they're traveling (true

---

*The study can be accessed at Upwork Research Institute's Future Workforce Index: https://www.upwork.com/research/future-workforce-index-2025.

story). Another tells you not to spend too much time on their project. You're exhausted from chasing payments, managing scope creep, pulling all-nighters, addressing interruptions, fielding criticisms and even personal attacks. All these drain your creative energy and require your time.

You're not told about any of this in design school.

FALLING INTO THE GAP

I experienced the gap myself soon after I graduated from an elite design school. Throughout my formal education I carried a vision of what my life would be like as a freelance creative. I'd be self-determined, free from time clocks, out from under the jurisdiction of others, and doing significant work for amazing clients. I'd be able to work from home and build my career while raising a family.

I had my portfolio and my degree, but no idea of how to achieve my goals of self-employment and self-determination. Some of my instructors had shared ways to promote my work to art directors and clients. So I followed their advice and landed a few paid projects very quickly.

My first professional project came just a few weeks after I sent out my first round of promotion pieces. It was a full page full color illustration for a small niche magazine. When my work was published, I discovered that changes had been made to the artwork — directly on it — which ruined it. (This was prior to the advent of computers as design tools, in the era of reflective artwork and process cameras.) Although I was paid promptly, I couldn't use the artwork or the printed piece in my portfolio. My signature was now on a badly crafted illustration.

Soon afterward, I was asked to design an ad for a fashion start-up. It was a rush job — they needed it the next day to meet a publication insertion deadline. I got it out the door on time and sent my invoice. The client never paid, never responded, and in fact, entirely disappeared. But my full page design was published in the widely-read, industry-leading fashion publication.

I have an extensive collection of true stories about the problems I ran into that I could share with you. It took me a long time dealing with recurring problems to realize that I was the common denominator in all my troubles. All the smaller problems pointed to one big problem: I lacked the essential business skills and mindset I needed to thrive as a freelance creative.

THE QUESTION THAT CHANGED EVERYTHING

One day, I asked myself a question that changed everything for me. Around 3:30AM, after having worked more than twenty hours straight making round after round of client-requested revisions on a tight deadline for a local lifestyle magazine, I was in tears. I was weary, fed up, frustrated, and angry. I asked myself, "Is it always going to be like this? It's not supposed to be this difficult!"

After I completed the project and sent it off to the client, I went to sleep. When I awoke I decided to do things differently. Pen and paper in hand (because I think better with those tools than with a keyboard,) I sat down and prayerfully took stock of my life and my business. I wrote a lot of notes.

I needed to protect my time. I needed to protect my work. I needed to protect my income sources. I needed to protect my creativity. I needed to protect my child from an overworked, frustrated, disillusioned single mom who had cried out in despair in the middle of the night. I made the decision to change — to shift gears, so to speak — and to learn how to run a business.

I went on a quest to find out what I needed to know and where to find those answers. I implemented what I learned. I started using written contracts. I started requiring payments in advance. I learned about copyright protection and intellectual property. I started qualifying clients before accepting their projects. I wrote out my values and non-negotiables. I figured out how to price my work appropriately and position on value instead of technique. I established and enforced business policies and systems.

This discovery, investigation and implementation was done over a few years' time, and not without trial and error. I had to figure out *what* I needed to know, *where* to get the answers, and *how* to *change my thinking*. The result is that now I work with high-value clients and create transformational work for them. I've now been freelancing for more than forty years. I've been able to pivot quickly in response to technological and economic shifts. I work when and where I want to. I've been able to diversify into content creation, media, teaching, and writing.

BRIDGING THE GAP

The gap between school and freelancing still exists and it's growing wider. One thing that's different now from when I graduated is that the economy has changed. There is no real security in working a full-time job for an employer. Currently there is a strong push toward entrepreneurship and self-determination. Independent designers, illustrators and photographers find themselves competing in a global marketplace where their fees are often undercut by crowd-sourcing and contests, freelance job platforms, and the lure of cheap AI solutions. So what is the creative, who has invested so much time, effort, and money, into developing their talents into marketable skills, to do?

Because the same problems I experienced remain common among freelancers, I began to write articles. I compiled what I learned from my own mistakes and successes into a blog, a course, a podcast, business coaching, and now this book, so that you don't have to learn everything through your own experience.

Thank you for reading this book, and for taking the time to carefully consider how you can apply what you learn from it to your own freelance business. My goal is to give you essential knowledge that's not taught in design school so you can build an independent creative business. With that knowledge and the confidence that comes with it, you can avoid many common problems freelancers encounter.

PART 1

MISSION

A STRONGLY FELT AMBITION OR CALLING

CHAPTER ONE

WHY CHOOSE FREELANCING?

Two foundational principles for working with multiple clients rather than one employer.

Freelancing is no longer simply taking on side jobs and booking gig work. It's a viable long term career option that allows you autonomy and flexibility in both work style and lifestyle. It represents a multi-billion dollar industry that allows you the freedom to craft your professional journey on your own terms, and make a living doing the work you enjoy.

I will say that freelancing isn't for the timid or tentative. Although you can take on side jobs while you're employed, freelancing full time is challenging, and scary. It involves knowledge and responsibilities you don't have to consider when you're an employee. Marketing, taxes, budgeting, accounting, branding and more all sit on the shoulders of the independent contractor.

While challenging and even unfamiliar if you're a creative, there's nothing you can't succeed at as a *creativepreneur* if you know what to do and how to do it. And that's the purpose of this book. It's a guide to help you leverage your creative skills into a thriving business.

Freelance creatives come in a variety of types — designers, illustrators, photographers, and copywriters, to name a few. Some of us have earned degrees while others are self-taught. Some work part time in addition to employment. Others are fully self-employed as independent contractors and consultants. Despite this diversity of creative skills and different paths of education and work product, there's one thing we all have in common: **We must learn business skills if we want to make a living from our creative work. If we desire to convert our passions into profits the way forward is to do business well.**

Generally, business skills are not taught in design school. Self-taught creatives don't naturally think about business concerns, either. We focus on the creative work. As a result, we can make significant, even tragic mistakes and suffer the consequences. We commit errors when we lack necessary knowledge.

In art school we learn how to make art. Our mindset is to be as creative and expressive as possible, to follow our passions and be fulfilled doing what we enjoy. We take classes to build our design vocabulary, technical know-how, and problem-solving skills. With the guidance of our teachers we build an amazing body of work. So design school helps us prepare our portfolios and then sends us out into the economy to build a career and make a living.

The problem is that having a stellar portfolio doesn't help you get along in the business world which is where your freelance clients exist. There's a gap between the creative and the business person, and both tend to avoid each other. Design school doesn't teach you how to bridge that gap. But it must be bridged if you intend to make a living on your own terms from your creative work.

What does it take to start freelancing? Where do you begin? And, equally important, what does it take to keep going?

Dear Creativepreneur, by picking up and reading this book, and then applying what you learn from it, you are building the foundations of that bridge between business and your creativity.

What's going to make or break you professionally is not how talented or skilled you are, or whether you earned a degree (I've never been asked to show my diploma or my resumé, by the way) but how well you do business. When you step into freelancing you become the owner of your creative business.

So, if you want to work independently, choose your clients, and enjoy the freedom of determining your own destiny; if you are entrepreneurial by nature and want to build your own brand as a business owner, you have to put on a business mindset. That's a foreign concept to the majority of creatives.

CHANGING YOUR MINDSET

Speaking the language of business and doing things in a businesslike manner is required when working with clients who own businesses and run organizations. Your goal as a freelance creative is to come alongside and help your clients achieve their goals which are business-based goals: They need to increase sales. They need to build awareness and influence. They need to attract more donors. They're pivoting in response to market trends and need to rebrand.

So if you pursue them with the idea of, "Look at this logo I made, isn't it pretty?" or, "How do you like the way I incorporated implied line in this photograph?" the client is going to be pushing back with the question, "How is that going to help increase my sales? How will that increase my competitive advantage? How is that going to help build my brand?"

A focus on creative work and fostering one's creative expression leads to problems for the unprepared. If you don't understand your clients' economic and reputation concerns you're in danger of being unable to sustain your business.

So where do you get business a training as a creative? My goal is to provide you with essential understanding. I've laid it out in four pillars: Mission, Mindset, Mechanics, and Message. By being mindful of all four you can build a business from your creative work.

TWO CORNERSTONE PRINCIPLES

There are a couple foundational principles you need to take hold of. The first one is that **business is transactional and transformational**. You're engaging in commerce and trading value for value. You're creating designs, illustrations, photographs, or copy that your clients will use to build their own businesses or organizations. They pay you to create the communication pieces they need. That's the transaction. It's a value-for-value exchange. Your clients are going to be comparing the amount of risk versus the amount of investment with you. So you can see that it's not all about things been pretty or artistically sound, or how skilled you are. From the business point of view your clients are looking for visual assets that they can use to grow their enterprises. That's the transformation.

The second foundational idea is that **you are in a service profession**. You provide for the needs of your clients. You're solving their problems. For example, a client reached out to me because they wanted to establish a nonprofit to connect youth who are aging out of the foster system with businesses who could train and employ them. The visual assets they needed were a logo, website, pitch deck, executive summary, and promotional pieces to attract and engage the business audience, the youth audience, and their sponsors — three audiences for this nonprofit. I had to keep all three groups in mind and create what was necessary to attract and engage each.

There was nothing about it that was about me. They selected me because of my approach to the project and because I was recommended by another client. In my process I was not looking at how can I make this more creative, or how can I express myself visually, or how can I bring my personality into this design. My goal was to create the work so that the client could achieve their goals. When you freelance, you serve your clients.

QUESTIONS TO ASK YOURSELF IF YOU'RE STARTING OUT

The first step in becoming a freelance creative is to assess your current circumstances, your desires, and consider what your ideal future might look like. What is your destination?

You may have already been considering these things, but it's important to be sober-minded and practical as you make an honest assessment. Owning and running a freelance business requires a different amount of risk than if you work for someone else. It's appropriate to consider whether starting a business is right for you at this point in time. In answering the questions below, be realistic about your skills, knowledge, strengths and weaknesses.

- Why do I want to freelance?
- What do I hope to achieve from freelancing?
- What are the foreseeable obstacles to my success?
- How much do I know about running a business?
- How much do I know about marketing and promotion?
- Who/what can I turn to for help?
- What resources are available to me?
- What is the quality of my portfolio?
- Is my work good enough (is it competitive)?
- Is there a need in the marketplace for what I do?
- What types of projects do I want to work on?
- What are my own strengths and weaknesses?
- How much money do I need to live and meet my obligations?
- Do I have savings?
- Do I have a backup plan just in case?
- What is my tolerance for risk?

QUESTIONS TO ASK YOURSELF IF YOU'RE ALREADY FREELANCING

If you've been freelancing for longer than one year, engaging in a self-assessment to discover the health of your business is recommended, and can be incorporated into you annual business planning. The following questions include purpose, areas of focus, ideal clients, skills, and satisfaction, all of which are key aspects of long-term success. Take time to reflect honestly and keep your answers in mind as you progress through the coming chapters.

- Why did I start freelancing?
- What are my areas of expertise?
- What am I good at?
- What is my differentiation/competitive advantage?
- What industry sectors do I currently serve?
- What industries do I prefer to serve?
- What is the average number of hours I work per week?
- What revenue did I generate last year?
- What is my projected revenue this current year?
- Am I charging enough?
- What can I do to increase my income?
- Which project was my most satisfying in the past year?
- Which client was the best to work with?
- What is working well in my business?
- What do I need to improve in my business?
- What do I need to stop doing/let go of?

Scheduling a critique of your business every quarter or every year (at minimum) helps keep things running smoothly. You can diagnose and troubleshoot your services, systems, finances and marketing. You'll be able to objectively identify strengths and weaknesses, and make necessary corrections.

We'll address many of these topics in the chapters ahead so you don't need to have set answers for everything at the moment. By answering these questions now you'll have an honest understanding of where you are, what you need to change, and a better potential for succeeding. And you'll get more benefit from this book.

CHAPTER TWO

THE VALUE OF YOUR CREATIVE WORK

Creative professions are service professions.

Contrary to opinions that art and design aren't viable professions, what we do as creatives has value in the world far beyond mere self-expression. One place we can go to understand our value as creatives is the Old Testament. Specifically, the book of *Exodus* where, out there in the vast wilderness between Egypt and the Promised Land (what is now known as Israel), the Creator empowered two creatives, Bezalel and Oholiab, with the ***wisdom, knowledge, and skill to design*** *artistic works*. He also endowed them with the ***ability to teach*** these skills to others. I want to use this passage to make a few very crucial points that should be pertinent to every creative.

First, **the work you do as a creative has value.** I'll return to this principle throughout this book. The first thing the Creator did was create. It's his very nature to create. He brought things into being that didn't previously exist. And he did it on purpose. The first act of God recorded in scripture is that he created. And he created for the good of others.

We do the same thing as freelance creatives: the products of our creative wisdom, knowledge and skill serve the people we work with. We create for their good, helping them achieve their business or organizational objectives. I could get into the reasons *why* God created, but that's for a different book.

Second, the account in Exodus is the very first **spiritual empowerment** — an *anointing* — by the divine being on human beings. There's no earlier anointing prior to this recorded in scripture. The empowerment was on artists and designers, not on accountants, doctors, attorneys, government leaders, shepherds, or any other profession considered *real* and *legitimate* work by our culture. Personally I believe that creativity's been hijacked, devalued, and deprecated, but that discussion is also for another book.

In scripture when an anointing was given there was specific and important work to be done. The anointing given to Oholiab and Bezalel didn't just empower their work, it declared their work necessary and valuable to their fellow human beings and to God. We can conclude that, if we possess the ability and desire to create, our work is inherently valuable and necessary.

It's also interesting to me that Jesus (Yeshua, Yehoshua) himself was by trade a carpenter — a skilled artisan. Up until he began to teach and preach he earned his living as a creative working with his hands and building things for people.

Third, consider that **everything is designed**. The layout of this book, the design of a coffee mug, the illustration on a box of breakfast cereal, your clothing, your automobile, toothbrush, and VR goggles are all designed. Can you name one thing in the built world that's not designed? Can you name one thing in the natural world that doesn't demonstrate design principles? Imagine how the world would be without the work of designers, photographers, illustrators, and copywriters.

Freelance creatives apply their skills and knowledge to help their clients achieve business goals. Our creative work is performed as a *service* to others, which makes it far more useful in the marketplace than mere self-expression.

If that is the case, should we not be encouraged to profit from our work and earn a living? Should we not be able to take care of ourselves, our families, our homes, and others through our work? Certainly we should. But we can't make a living by our talent alone.

DEFINITIONS

If you're a freelance creative, you're a self-employed, independent contractor who serves clients, as distinct from creating and selling products. You're a type of *creativepreneur.* Let's look at this further:

Creativity means to bring something into existence. The creative process involves recognizing needs or problems to solve, developing and testing ideas, refining and tweaking, and creating a resulting product.

An **entrepreneur** is someone who organizes and operates a business or enterprise, and undertakes a high degree of risk in doing so.

An **enterprise** is a difficult project or undertaking that requires considerable effort, most often involving *economic activity.*

Based on these dictionary definitions, we define a **creativepreneur** as someone who builds a profit-making business around a creative passion, mission, or purpose.

A **freelancer** is a person who serves multiple clients at different times and concurrently rather than or in addition to being *employed* at one company.

THE VALUE OF WORK

Work is a noble activity. Work is defined as *mental and/or physical effort expended in order to achieve a purpose or result.* All work is necessary and meaningful if we regard it as *service* to others. Work is the means by which we provide for ourselves and help other at the same time. This is true whether we're employed or freelance.

Not everyone understands the value of creative work or the desire to be self-employed. The important thing is that you understand how your creative work serves the world, and why you prefer independence over employment. These concepts are foundational for any creative who wants to build a business from their creative work.

CHAPTER THREE

THE IMPORTANCE OF KNOWING WHY

You need to identify what's at stake.

I often reflect on how blessed I am to be independent creative able to determine where, when, how, and with whom I work. I also consider why I'm a *creativepreneur* instead of a staff designer on someone else's payroll. I think about the WHY a lot. My WHY is what keeps me going. It's my primary motivation.

Notice I said *consider why* instead of *wonder why.* I've moved far beyond the question, "Why am I doing this?" Rather than trying to figure that out, I simply need to remind myself of it. It's crucial to know why we've chosen to do something and chosen to not do something else instead.

When we feel validated in what we're doing — a client praises our work, a project turns out successfully, we get paid well and on time, a favorite client recommends us to their colleagues — we see the good results of what we're doing. In those cases, our WHY appears obvious.

On the flip side there are those other times — we lose a client, we don't see hoped-for results, we're given a poor critique, we're just not having fun anymore — when knowing why we're doing this thing becomes crucial for persevering. We need to focus in on our purpose in order to keep going.

WHAT IS THE WHY?

Your WHY is that deeply-held, personal motivation for what you pursue. For example, my WHY includes freedom. Freedom is one of my primary motivators both professionally and personally. Freedom — the ability to do the work I want to do, to choose who I work with, to set my own schedules, to go where I want to when I want to, to integrate work and family life — is a primary reason I chose to be self-employed.

For a time early on in my career I was a salaried employee and freelanced on the side. But working for someone else just didn't fit me. There were times as a freelancer when I seriously considered returning to a full time salaried position, but I kept coming back to the freedom issue. That motive, among others, has kept me moving forward and on track as a *creativepreneur*. I believe I've had far more impact working with clients than I would have had working for an employer. The freedom motivation has kept me independent. It's a non-negotiable.

One thing I've learned and will pass on to you is this: **Until you identify your WHY you won't be able to get clear about your WHATS and HOWS.** If you don't discover your WHY, your chances of long-term success are reduced. Why? Any worthy goal will be met with resistance. If you have lofty goals for your life (hopefully you do), you will go against the tide along the way. You'll experience opposition, road blocks, fatigue. The only motivator you have for pushing through problems is your WHY.

To uncover your WHY, begin by asking yourself, what is the destination you need to get to? Why does it matter to you? **What is at stake – for you and those connected to you – if you do not accomplish your goals?** Freelance creatives often set solid, realistic goals but don't achieve them because they're not motivated by their WHY.

The secret of the WHY is that it is personal to you. It's not about being helpful to others, although that should be a result. **Your WHY is all about what's in it for you.** If you don't have a stake in it, it's not your WHY.

HOW TO DISCOVER YOUR WHY

Generally, people focus on completing actions and tasks. They fill up a to do list and get things done and feel satisfied that they've accomplished what they set out to do each day. But a sense of satisfaction and fulfillment will not necessarily drive you to reach your destination. You need to know what your destination is — your preferred future — in order to know how to get there. What is the grand idea, the big picture for your life? How does entrepreneurship — specifically, freelancing — get you there?

It's crucial to know why you want to freelance. What is the driving motivator within you that indicates you're more of an entrepreneur than an employee? Consider what's important to you. What are your values? What are your non-negotiables — those things that are not open to discussion or modification? What do you imagine your ideal life to look like? Envisioning the destination will keep you motivated and moving forward. Otherwise, what will keep you going when (not if) trouble shows up? The apostle Paul wrote about running a race to win the prize. *Do you not know that those who run in a race all run, but one receives the prize? Run in such a way that you may obtain it.* — 1 CORINTHIANS 9:24 NKJV.

What's your prize? To uncover the answer, these are questions you can ask yourself and write out your answers:

What do you want to be known for? In other words, how do you want people to remember you? What outcome do you want for your work and life as a whole? How are you wired? What motivates you? These questions center on you as a unique, one-of-a-kind person. It's necessary to think of creative work, building a business, and building a life as a single complete thing, not several things that you have to manage side by side. It's one integrated whole made up of different parts that need to work together. What do you want to be known and remembered for?

What is most important to you? What matters most? When considering your work and personal life as a whole, what are your priorities and non-negotiables? This isn't about what's important to your spouse or partner, your kids, your parents, your employer. It's about you. No one else can decide your non-negotiables for you.

I was on the phone with my sister-in-law a number of years ago when I first realized what my non-negotiables are. I don't remember exactly the topic of our conversation, but it must have centered on life purpose, divine calling, and such. In the course of our conversation she asked me what's most important to me. I blurted out my response before I could think about it: "Truth and freedom." That was a divine revelation for me, because I'd never considered the question before.

Once I made this declaration, things began to fall into place for me simply because I understood what drove me. My desire for truth keeps me connected to who I believe is the source of truth. My desire for freedom underscores how I live my life.

How can you get from where you are right now to where you want to be? What steps do you need to take, what paths will you follow? What do you need to change? What should you let go of?

YOUR WHY MAKES YOUR GOALS MEANINGFUL

When you figure out your WHY, it's time to map your path of travel to that destination. Remember that achieving your WHY and reaching success as you've defined it happens by taking a series of steps in a predetermined direction.

For each of your goals, there exists a reason. You don't need to fabricate it because it already exists. Here's how you discover it:

1. **Keeping your WHY in mind, write down three specific goals you want to accomplish during the next 90 days.** Be specific and make them measurable (you will know when you've accomplished them). Include a due date. For example:

- Over the next 3 months, I will read 6 books about business and marketing.
- I will send a marketing email to 10 prospective clients once each week for the next 12 weeks.
- By [date] I will research business coaching opportunities and choose one to engage.

Also, be sure you make your goals relevant to you. Don't base them on others' expectations.

2. **For each goal, identify and list 3–5 personal motivations.** Ask yourself, "Why does this matter? Why is it important to me? What is at stake?" You're not listing tasks here. Your focus is on the reasons for the goal. For example:

Goal: By (a date 14 days from today), I will research business coaching opportunities:
√ Because I need to learn from someone who has a successful freelance business
√ Because I want to learn how to build a successful freelance business and quit my day job.
√ Because I want to avoid common problems that freelancers experience
√ Because I need to be able to support myself and my family with my freelance business

You can apply this exercise for any goal, whether personal or business. If you cannot think of at least three personal motivations for each of your specific goals, carefully consider if it is indeed the right goal. Your goals should be both emotionally compelling and intellectually relevant. They should be significant enough that pursuing them will change you. Remember what's at stake if you don't get them done.

3. **Prioritize your motivations** in order of importance. In the scenario above, the fourth reason is the primary reason.

4. **Schedule your goals** on your calendar and display your calendar in an easily accessible place (sticky note, app, spreadsheet) so that you can refer to it and follow through consistently. Track your progress toward each goal.

THE BIGGER QUESTION

There is much at stake if you don't plan your steps and set your goals. You will not take the necessary steps without being motivated to do so. A number of goals you set will require some sort of sacrifice, so you need to consider what's at stake. If you want to accomplish something, there will be a cost to it. One example of sacrificing something in order to achieve a goal is choosing to cancel your streaming subscriptions and eating at home instead of going to restaurants so that you can pay off debt quickly.

Jesus' cautionary words are a fitting mandate for us freelance creatives: *"But don't begin until you count the cost. For which of you, desiring to build a tower, does not first sit down and count the cost, whether he has enough to complete it? Otherwise, when he has laid a foundation and is not able to finish, all who see it begin to mock him, saying, 'This man began to build and was not able to finish.'"*
— Luke 14:28–30 ESV

For example, if your goal is to work with a business coach to help build your business, the costs involved are financial, time, focus, and accountability. How will you pay for the coaching sessions? What will you forego in order to have the funds required? What activities will you set aside while you're working with the coach? How willing are you to receive and act on the teaching and counsel you'll receive (are you teachable or stubborn?) How will you guard your time with family and friends so that you are able to focus on the work of building your business?

As you move forward with a goal, you will experience resistance. Remembering your motivations — your WHY — will propel you forward in spite of opposition. Your WHY makes the sacrifices worth the effort and the boundaries you establish in order to get it done.

CHAPTER FOUR

COUNTING THE COST

Advantages and Disadvantages of Freelancing

In the previous chapter I shared about knowing your WHY, and touched on counting the cost before you begin. In this chapter we'll explore the costs, benefits and risks of independent contracting.

Freelancing provides more freedom than any other type of work structure. Along with that freedom come the responsibilities of ownership and reputation. When we choose to freelance, we are choosing to be self-reliant and responsible for our own destinies. We define success on our own terms.

Just as there are wonderful aspects to freelancing, there are harsh realities as well. As with anything, to enjoy the freedoms we need to pay the price for them. Just as freedom comes with a cost, freelancing is not a free ride to success.

THE ADVANTAGES OF FREELANCING

You can start freelancing with minimal expenses. The costs to start a business are minimal to non-existent, depending upon what you already have on hand in equipment, work space, and connectivity. If you have creative desire and some technical skills, you have what you need to work with clients.

You can do more than one thing. You can illustrate and design. You can be a social media marketer and a photographer. You can serve clients and also be a maker who sells products.

You can start part-time and develop into full time. It's easy to begin a side business while you're employed by taking on freelance projects. This strategy allows you to test the waters before fully committing, maintaining your employment as a safety net. At the point when you're ready to leave the full-time job, it can be a smooth transition if you've prepared well.

You can work where you want to and when you want to. From home, at an office or co-working space, at your favorite coffee shop, at the library, on the road in your converted van. Since you are not clocking in and out during an employer's business hours, you get to determine your own schedule. As long as you meet the agreed-upon project deadlines, it doesn't matter when or where you do the work.

You can work on what you want to. You have the freedom to say "no" to a project or client and not have to take on something you don't want to do or aren't confident about. This means you can enjoy your work as much as you enjoy your life aside from work, seeking and accepting projects that are fulfilling for you. For many freelancers, our work is fun and we actually look forward to Mondays.

THE DOWNS OF FREELANCING

Inconsistent income. Even after you become established with a steady stream of clients, you will earn more in some months than in others. Having money in savings and a spending plan (a budget) will enable you to pay your expenses during leaner months. Ideally, you should build and maintain enough in savings to cover three months worth of living expenses to offset times of sparse income.

You will pay a higher percentage of income tax than if you are employed. Employers pay 50% of an employee's income taxes in the form of payroll taxes. As a self-employed person, you are responsible for paying all of your income taxes, making estimated tax payments to the IRS every quarter. The amount you owe will be determined by your net profit from your business.

You need to get out and market yourself, network, and make connections. You can't acquire clients unless you go looking for them and make yourself known. Freelancers are often quiet and introverted when it comes to self-promotion. This must be overcome in order to attract clients. Do what is necessary to get the word out about your creative services. This is part of counting the cost — sacrificing your personal comfort for the sake of your business and ideal future.

You will work more than 40 hours in a week. The ability to manage creative projects and business activities requires you to plan and manage your time well. Don't be deceived into thinking that you will come and go by the clock. It's your choice to work five extra hours on a Friday evening in order to have all of Saturday off from your work, or to take Friday off and do some work over the weekend. It's a choice to take on a project that will have you working sixteen hours in a day and through the weekend to meet a client's deadline. Time is a cost of being a freelance business owner.

Especially if you have a spouse or partner and/or children, you'll need to budget your time for your business and your personal life so that you are fully present for both when you need to be. You'll need to guard your family and personal time from your business activities, and conversely guard your business and professional time from your family. You will work a lot of hours as a business owner, but have an amazing amount of flexibility.

Not all clients are trustworthy. It's sad to say, but true. There are difficult, over-demanding, and non-communicative clients out there. There are clients who disappear and don't pay you. Therefore put systems and policies in place in order to minimize and avoid these troubles as much as possible. Look out for "red flags". Establish criteria for recognizing your ideal client and seek those who fit the criteria.

The *free* in freelancing relates to *being* free — to not being tied down to any one commitment, set schedule or working relationship. It does not mean you work for free. It is not license to do whatever you feel like doing if you are serious about building a freelance career. You will not earn a living if you neglect the necessary work.

Think of freelancing more as doing what you need to do, but in your own way and schedule. If you take care of business well, you can build a life that balances work and personal time, pay your bills, and pursue your interests and passions. Start by being realistic about the entire freelance picture.

CHAPTER FIVE

IDENTIFY THE GAP

Focus on the objectives instead of your talent.

Whether it's illustration, photography, design, or copy writing we creative freelancers are in a service profession. But what exactly is our role as professional service providers? Is it to take e-commerce product photos? Is it to paint a magazine cover? Is it to build a website? Is it to design a logo? We're not creating artwork and designs for our clients. We create the results — the intended outcomes — that those things will achieve.

When working with my students and advising on brand strategy with clients I often share a story about a person who walks into a hardware store to buy some lumber and a power drill. On the surface he's going there to buy tools and materials. Digging deeper, we understand that earlier that day, his beloved Great Dane, Ittybitty, decided to chase a member of the local squirrel population through the backyard fence which now lies flat on top of the neighbor's petunia patch. The reason for making the hardware store run is to buy the tools and materials needed to repair the fence. Repairing the fence will mend the relationship with the very distraught neighbor. In this case, going to the hardware store isn't about buying tools. It's about relationship management.

Let's translate that concept to your role as a service provider. You don't actually create things. Your role is to create *solutions*. You design, draw, photograph or write in order to solve business problems for your clients. As discussed in Chapter 2, that's where the value of our work exists.

UNDERSTAND THE CLIENT'S PURPOSE

Most of the time, clients and prospects will reach out when they have a need they can't or don't want to fulfill on their own, or they don't know how. If they don't have a need, there's no reason for them to seek you out. The client's journey from their problem to your solution typically looks like this:

- They become aware something's not working for their business.
- They realize they don't know how to solve the problem, or don't want to or can't take it on themselves.
- They start searching for someone who can provide a solution.
- In their search they land on your website and choose you.
- They work with you for a successful outcome.
- They tell others about how you helped them.

For our marketing and outreach purposes, we should be focused on their needs instead of our talents. We **identify the gap between where our clients are and where they want to be**, and then step into that gap to close it. That makes us problem-solvers. Consider these scenarios:

A canine companions organization has their annual fundraising event coming up and needs to invite their current donor base, and also convince new donors and patrons to not only attend but also materially support their cause. They also want their clients (disabled veterans and similarly-challenged adults) to attend with their service dogs. They reach out to a designer to create and implement an event identity and touch points that will stir hearts and influence both audiences (the donors and the clients) to support the cause. The designer is asked to handle everything from initial concept through implementation and mailing. The ultimate goal of the design work isn't the event, but to raise awareness and funds to obtain, train, and place more service dogs that will make life more convenient and comfortable for challenged people.

A start-up luxury home textiles business needs a product photographer who can effectively showcase the quality and beauty of their bespoke 100% organic cotton bath towels and robes. The photos will be deployed on their e-commerce site and on social media channels. The end goal is to increase sales so that the business can scale and provide jobs for more people.

A first-time author is skeptical of the low aesthetic quality of many self-published books and seeks a designer-illustrator who's able to develop their project cover-to-cover, design for high value, prepare the book layout files for print and ebook formats, and guide them through the self-publishing process.

An entrepreneur intends to build an exclusive online community for fellow entrepreneurs and needs a membership website, apps, and visual assets for branding and marketing. The purpose isn't these assets themselves, or even building a community platform. It's the shared knowledge, encouragement, connections, and support that people will gain through participation.

Each of these actual, real-life situations presents a need that we creatives can satisfy. Our purpose is not about creating layouts, writing copy, or photographing products, but what those things will accomplish for our clients.

When we approach our own marketing by focusing on how creative, innovative, low-cost, and successful we are, we're not attractive to prospects looking for solutions to their business problems. **If we don't acknowledge their needs, they won't ask us to solve their problems.** But when we identify the communication and marketing problems we can solve, and *position* on being the helpful solution, we stand out from the usual "Hire me because I'm really creative!" and, "I'm the best!" and, "I'm the cheapest!" approaches.

Who are your clients? What problems do you solve for them? Schedule some time this week to list those problems and how you can solve them. Then, based on your list, create marketing content that positions you as a creative problem-solver. Since this exercise is a very appropriate use of artificial intelligence tools in your business, why not go ahead and use them for this exercise. Write a detailed prompt that describes your target audience, your marketing goals, key message as a creative problem-solver, and posting schedule, and ask for hook (headline) ideas that will "stop the scroll." Then scrutinize and assess the results, tweak what needs tweaking, adjust your calendar, and deploy the content. Edit your social media profiles and your website's home page copy to reflect your newly-crafted results-based offer.

CHAPTER SIX

DESTINY AND DETOURS

Detours can be useful for preparation, refining, strengthening skills, and gaining perceptions and insights.

Everything you do in your life adds up to your whole life. As an independent creative professional, you have *all* your experiences, knowledge and skill to draw on to create your success and arrive at your destination.

But the road to your destination is not a straight, smooth super-highway. There are twists and turns. There are long, boring stretches. And sometimes you'll end up on a side road.

I'm going to use the concept of a *road trip* as a metaphor for the freelance experience. One thing we can encounter on a road trip is a *detour.* A detour is defined as *a long, round-about route usually taken to avoid something or taken when the intented route is closed or otherwise unavailable.*

HOW DO YOU END UP ON A DETOUR?

Early in my career, I worked at a few jobs that were entirely unrelated to what I studied in school. My intent was to freelance on the side and pay my bills with day jobs until I got enough clients to quit and freelance full time.

So I worked in retail for a time. I worked as a bank teller. For a few years I worked in administration at a prestigious art college. But none of these jobs were my destiny. And I knew it.

Even so, each of these jobs in turn became my focus. I stopped creating. I came home fatigued at the end of the day, drained of all energy to do any creative work. I had no time or energy to make cold calls, send out my marketing promotions, or develop new work. My freelance side hustle wasn't hustling.

This continued for a few years. I lost passion, focus, and drive to pursue my destiny. While I was successful at these jobs, I wasn't satisfied. I had a deep down sense that I was on the wrong road but didn't know where the offramp was. I found myself despairing of ever having the life I dreamed of. I actually started to accept my situation, and convince myself that I must have misunderstood my purpose. I could always pursue my creative work as a hobby as so many do, but that idea fell short in terms of the value of my work and its relevance to others.

Those early jobs were *detours* — side trips. While they solved my immediate needs of paying my bills and supporting my child, they had nothing to do with my purpose (my divine calling — my WHY.) I was on side roads that led me away from what I was convinced was my destination.

Can you relate? I know so many creatives who have found themselves having to *get a real job* in order to live.

DETOURS ARE DISTRACTIONS

Detours are alternate routes you take when the main road isn't available. The idea of taking a detour is that you continue moving in a forward direction and eventually return to the main road.

Detours can be full of adventure, but getting back to where you need to be can be a challenge. A detour can even look like the main road if you've been on it long enough. In other words, you settle in and just keep driving, hoping you'll end up somewhere. But detours aren't your destiny.

I'm recalling the life of Joseph (GENESIS 37–50.) He had a destiny, and he knew it. But through some dubious choices, he was sold by his disgruntled siblings to some slave traders and ended up miles — physically and emotionally — from where he expected to be. He held onto his WHY while on this detour. He was falsely accused, imprisoned, and when eventually released was reunited to his destiny, saving millions of people. I often think about his mindset during the prison years — did he ever let go of his dreams?

Back to my story: I'd been paralleling my main road long enough, working the art school day job and believing that it was the right thing because I enjoyed it and it paid the bills.

One day, I had a sudden, unexpected reality check that the detour I was on was completely wrong. This is how it happened. On a Friday morning in early September I walked in to my office at the art college and started working as usual. An hour later I got a call from the college president's office. He wanted to see me.

So at about noon that same day, I walked out of my office for the last time, carrying my stuff in a box, having been given an ample severance package, referrals, and letters of recommendation from the president. The reason? My department was going to be reorganized, and I no longer had a job. My regular paycheck and "secure" job no longer existed. I had no control in the situation.

It was on the drive home that I decided to no longer take the side roads. I'd get back on the main highway and pursue my destiny, doing what I set out to do in the first place. The following Monday I started freelancing full time, and teaching part time on the side.

Looking back, I was surprised that I didn't panic. Instead, I had the sense that although everything had suddenly changed without warning, everything was going to be okay. I believe Joseph had the same mindset. What about you?

CIRCUMSTANCES CREATE DETOURS

Have you ever noticed that, when you decide to go for a big goal, opposition shows up? Life creates road blocks and hazards that we have to navigate. Our plans are interrupted. Our efforts are thwarted. We end up settling for less than we planned and hoped for.

In settling for less than we're called to, we become weary. We get caught up in living and working, and lose sight of our destination. Or we give in to others' expectations. It seems easier — it seems less selfish or creates less friction — to give up on our dreams and take an expedient road — a detour.

DETOURS ARE NOT WASTED TIME

You could lament the time on a detour as time wasted. You can think, "Why didn't I do things differently?" You can beat yourself up over losing your way. But there's a better way to look at those choices, and that's what I want you to do. Be like Joseph. Choose the right mindset.

Consider this: A detour might be necessary to reach your intended destination. The time you spend on a side road is not wasted unless you decide it is. What I learned during my time on my side routes proved invaluable when I got returned to the main road. I had learned things while on detour that helped me succeed in my creative work, in doing business, and in working with people. They propelled me toward my destiny.

Likewise, the detours you take can be useful for preparation, refinement, strengthening skills, changing perceptions, and gaining insights. These all increase your ability to support and stand up under the weight of your destiny. For example:

- My short stint working in retail taught me how to serve a diverse spectrum of people.
- While a bank teller, I learned that money is a tool, not a goal.
- During my time working at an art college, I learned business and sales copy writing, how to train and mentor people, how

to manage multiple complex projects concurrently, and how to market.

Everything I learned on the side route became part of my skill set which I still continue to use in serving clients and growing my creative business.

EXPERIENCES ARE TEACHERS

Even if we know exactly what our destiny is — our life purpose, what we're called to do — we don't start out fully capable of doing it. In fact, we begin with very little ability at all. Training and discipline are necessary to build skill, competence, and confidence. Experience is necessary to gain wisdom.

You need to build the ability to carry what you were made to do. If you're not strong enough to carry something, it will defeat you.

If you take the perspective that a detour was useful — it kept you safe, it taught you new skills, it strengthened you, it provided a different perspective — you won't consider it a waste of time. It prepared you for the greater work you have yet to do.

Don't spend your energy feeling sorry, disappointed, or bitter about the detours you've been on. Instead, look at those experiences from a different point of view. What did you learn? How are you stronger? How are you better skilled? How are you more confident?

Consider and record your thoughts: What detours have you taken in the past? What did you learn from them? How are you better off because of them? How will you implement them in developing your creative business?

CHAPTER SEVEN

SET GOALS, NOT RESOLUTIONS

Big results require big goals.

Do you make New Year's resolutions every year? Have you kept any of them? What's your track record for keeping your resolutions for more than a month?

What would you like to accomplish? What do you want to change? Where do you see yourself twelve months from today? What do you want to be doing two years from now?

GOALS ARE NOT RESOLUTIONS

Simply making resolutions does not accomplish anything. If we are serious and determined about making changes or accomplishing something, we must do more than simply resolve to do it. We must make it specific, schedule it, and then follow through on it.

Do you want to launch your freelance business this year? Do you want a different type of client? Do you want to build your creative expertise? Do you want to level up? Don't wait. Start on it now.

Write out your goals. God instructed Habakkuk to write the vision down so that it was clear and actionable: *Then the LORD answered me and said: "Write the vision and make it plain on tablets, that he may run who reads it."* — HABAKKUK 2:2 NKJV

Why should you write down your goals? Because you're more likely to get them done than if you don't. Human memory is untrustworthy. When you write something down you don't need to keep it in your head. The paper remembers it for you, and you won't lose it among all your other thoughts. If it's written you can display it in a prominent place and view it regularly. Studies* have revealed that successful people write things down, especially if it's important, meaningful, or inspirational. Your goals are important, meaningful, and inspirational. So get them down on paper. Or in an app.

One key to accomplishing anything is to **decide** to do it, and then to **schedule** it. It's easy to write something down and then do nothing about it. You will not take action on an idea until you **make a commitment** to it by writing it down and scheduling it in your calendar. Remember, the reason God told Habakkuk to write it down was so that one could take action on it. The point is the action. You will not change anything until you take action. Because we're holistic people, **ideas, plans and actions work together.** A goal that is only written down is a resolution — an idea. An idea that is written and scheduled is a goal. Placing action steps onto your calendar will motivate you to move forward. **Calendars are motivators**.

In Chapter 6 I discussed the concept of *destiny*. Think of a goal as a destination — a place you want to go to. When you complete a string of actions that move you toward that destination, you will achieve your goal. Getting from where you are to your objective requires time, navigation, and fuel. It's easy to sit in the back seat

---

*Here is one study: Matthews, Gail, "The Impact of Commitment, Accountability, and Written Goals on Goal Achievement" (2007). Psychology | Faculty Presentations. 3. https://scholar.dominican.edu/psychology-faculty-conference-presentations/3

and allow someone else to drive, but then you're at the mercy of the driver, going where they want to go. As a solo creative, you are the driver. You can idle, burning up fuel and accomplishing nothing, or you can determine where you want to go, get into gear, go forward, build momentum, and accelerate.

Another key to accomplishing your goals is to have a grander purpose for your goals. The grander purpose is your WHY (Chapter 3.) When your goals are extensions of your WHY they gain relevance and meaning.

One of my goals was to completely pay off debt and be entirely free from owing anyone anything. That purpose under-girded the smaller goals that led up to it: pay off the car, pay off the mortgage, pay off consumer debt, plan my spending, and such. Why did I want to get my debt paid off completely? Ultimately, my purpose was to be free. *...the borrower is slave to the lender.* — PROVERBS 22:7. Freedom is one of my values and is foundational to my WHY.

MAKE YOUR GOALS AUDACIOUS

When you want big results you need to set big goals. Big goals are scary. They're scary because you have to make changes in order to accomplish them. Once accomplished, you're in a very different place than you were when you started out.

In general, people set small goals — tasks and action steps. They write out and schedule many small things and are satisfied that they've done everything on a to-do list. They're busy with these minor tasks, but ineffective in changing their circumstances.

So set big goals. It's necessary to understand the difference between small actions (tasks) and big goals. Starting a sustainable, profitable freelance business is a big goal. Writing a book is a big goal. Buying a home is a big goal. Posting on social media every day is a task.

Instead of planning out numerous small actions and tasks to check off, decide on a few audacious, seemingly impossible, goals. Then write out the sequences of steps (tasks, actions) you need to complete in order to achieve those big goals.

HOW TO ACHIEVE YOUR GOALS

An effective approach to achieving your goals includes:

1. Setting appropriate goals. Appropriate goals move you along the road toward your destination. They are appropriate and fitting for you, and will provide both personal and professional reward. Also, others will benefit when you reach a goal. People need what you have to offer. You can't offer anything without reaching some goals.

2. Beginning where you are. You may not be where you were hoping to be at this point in time, but no matter. Where you are is the best place to start. Where you are gives you clarity on what to do next.

3. Beginning with what you have. Don't put off forward motion until you feel ready, or until you can afford it, or until you have all your ducks in a row. (It is my observation that ducks never do line up.) Step out in faith. Use what you have now: your knowledge, your skill, your experience, your desire. Do what you know to do. Build from there.

4. Scheduling your goals. Give each goal a deadline. Then, break each down into smaller steps and add the steps to your calendar, giving each a due date. On the day you have planned to do a step, do it.

5. Tell someone. Share your goals with someone who's an encouragement to you — friend, family member, business coach, fellow freelancer. Telling others what you want to accomplish establishes accountability. And, since you've let the other person know what you're up to, you have someone to talk with about the goal and challenges you face, and who will encourage you.

START NOW AND KEEP GOING

Accomplishing goals and achieving your purpose is the result of taking a series of small steps in the right direction. So take the next small step. Step out in faith, with determination to keep going, one step at a time. After completing the first step move on to the next.

The more consistently you take action on your goals, the more momentum you build, and your freelance road trip becomes exciting because things are getting done. You build competence and confidence with each accomplishment, no matter how small. Each step and goal is a mile markers on your road to achieving your ultimate purpose.

Write down an audacious (willing to take bold, risky actions) goal, something huge and even life-changing that you've intended to do but haven't gotten around to yet. Assign it a due date. Add the due date to your calendar. Schedule one to three small action steps you can take toward it over the next seven days. Then be sure to follow through and do those actions on the days you scheduled them. This will start your forward momentum. Once you've completed these initial steps, schedule more steps for the next week, and every week after that until you reach your goal. When you've accomplished the goal, set another one. As you get your goals done you'll enjoy the accomplishments and inspiration to keep going.

CHAPTER EIGHT

VALUES ARE YOUR GPS

How we work is more important than the kind of work we do.

Let's begin with the premise that design, illustration and photography are *service* professions, and that being a professional means you're in business. You're making a living by doing something that you love to do which ultimately helps a business or organization do what it does.

We each operate best in our sweet spot — that which we love and do best because we are naturally made for it. We each know our own bent, and look to others — even our clients — to support us rather than hinder us in our endeavors. The fact that you love your work does not make you any less a professional or your creative practice any less a business. If you're a solo creative, **how your clients understand your role in their success is crucial to your success**. As a soloist, it's easy to blur the boundaries when your client asks you to assist or produce in a way that's inappropriate. We'll often accept these odd requests to be nice, but accepting or acquiescing opens the door to distractions and false perceptions.

DEFINE YOUR ROLE

My clients' understanding of my role needs to be constantly adjusted if I'm going to do what I do best. This necessitates that I clearly define my role, and not let clients define it for me. They'll bring assumptions, perceptions, and expectations based on their prior experiences, and I have to gently but firmly correct them. It's the same for you.

Why is this important? The problem of perceptions arises when we function in ways that don't align with our values, roles and services offered. For example, I've been referred to by clients as an IT person, a publicist, a marketing consultant, a print broker, and a web developer. I am none of these. I've been asked to salvage files from a crashed hard drive, to manage a client's Facebook page, and to set up Outlook on a client's laptop. I was asked to look after a client's dog and water their plants while they were out of town. These things are not among my service offerings. They are distractions from my creative work. If I agreed to do these things, I would have operated against my values and my brand would have been harmed.

PERCEPTION MANAGEMENT

A colleague of mine, Jerry, was key in teaching me this lesson. It was a couple decades ago that I contacted him one morning because I'd received a request from a business woman who wanted the colors on her logo changed. I didn't have the time to do this very small thing, which I anticipated becoming an on-going back and forth until she was satisfied, if ever. When I hesitated in saying no, she asked if I could refer someone. So I asked Jerry if he might take it on. His reply was simple, "That's not what I do."

That one simple, clear, indomitable answer had quite a profound impact on me. Up to that point I had been willing to take on work I didn't really want to do or shouldn't do. This realization changed my understanding and point of view. From that moment on, I began following Jerry's example to graciously decline work, and doing so gave me the courage to say no to unsuitable projects. By saying no to low-value work, I was better able to attract and say yes to high-value projects. And I also realized I needed to operate on the basis of my values without compromise.

We may think our role in working with clients is well-defined and the line is clearly drawn. When we cross our own lines of demarcation the client is confused and forms the wrong idea. It can also happen that they just come with a wrong idea of what a creative does. Either way, *perception management* is necessary. If we allow others to define our work based on their convenience or expectations, we'll find ourselves expected to provide and perform in ways we can't or don't want to. This problem occurs often with creative soloists, but businesses and organizations can also experience it.

How do we manage perceptions and expectations? We begin by defining our roles and underlying *values* — those non-negotiable principles and standards of behavior which are founded on one's world view. These are a few of my values, which are based on my personal paradigms:

Creativity. I create with intention and intelligence. God is the source of my creativity and primary inspiration no matter who I serve.

Service. I'm not an artist. I'm a creative who serves clients by solving their business and communications problems.

Excellence. I watch over details. I'm well-trained, experienced, and continually self-educate. I consistently work to improve and refine my craft.

Integrity. I act in accordance with my beliefs and world view. I turned down high-profile clients offering lucrative projects if they are contrary to my deeply-held beliefs.

Initiative. I keep an eye on business, culture, and politics so that I can anticipate next moves for my clients and my own business.

Focus. I accept projects that propel me forward — work that leads to better and more significant work.

Your values are foundational to your brand, your business policies and how you manage projects and clients. Working in alignment with your values means you won't accept every prospective client, every project offered, or perform outside your sweet spot. You can more easily say "No" to requests and projects that don't fit. You will ensure that others perceive you correctly, get the kind of work you want to do, and attract the clients you want to work with.

Take some time to reflect on these questions: Have you been asked to perform work that is outside the scope of your creative services? If you obliged, how did the client's understanding of your role change as a result? How did you address it? What did you do, or will you do, differently going forward?

If you haven't already written out your values, now is a good time to do that. Make a list of your non-negotiable standards of behavior and principles by which you live. Write down five or six values to begin with. Then define each for yourself. For example, if creativity is one of your values, what does that mean to you? Values should be relevant and meaningful to you or you won't consistently live and work by them. Once you've defined them, review your business policies to make sure they align. For example, if communication is one of your values, are you using written contracts and proposals? Do you follow up every conversation with a summary email?

CHAPTER NINE

THE ROLES OF VISION AND MISSION

How to succeed in business for the long haul.

You can go into business, acquire clients, and make a living without searching out a greater purpose for your work. But if you have a vision, you'll be sustained in your work through the ups and downs. You'll experience less doubt about your work and role. You'll have a business that is more than transactional (focused on making money.) In contrast, your business will be transformational by affecting peoples' lives for the better.

Your vision and mission are a compass that guides your decisions and help you navigate through all sorts of circumstances. They're the basis for your goals and business objectives, the foundation for your values, and reminders of your purpose as a creative. They provide you with clear direction to keep you on the straight and narrow path toward your destination.

It's easy to think that mission and vision statements are useful only for corporations and mid-sized businesses with numerous employees, but they're also quite necessary for the independent creative. Making the effort to consider your WHY and express it through vision and mission statements allows you to position your business strategically relative to your competitors.

THE BENEFITS OF VISION AND MISSION STATEMENTS

Focus. Mission and vision clarify what you're doing, why you're doing it, and its benefit to the people you work with. They also define what you don't do, so that you don't get stuck providing services you don't want to offer.

Discernment. Having a vision and mission help guard against making wrong decisions about your business and ideal clients. It's not unusual for a prospective client to think you do things that you don't offer. For example, for a number of years I worked with a client who became comfortable enough in our working relationship to request that I set up his booth at a trade show. This would have involved transporting all his gear and rented equipment, setting it up, and then taking it down and transporting it all back. I was able to decline this request because that's not what I do.

Positioning. Your vision and mission help to categorize your services. For example, if you define your business as web design focus, you're not positioning as a brand strategist or publication designer. If you want to provide web design, brand strategy, and publication design, you'll take a different position and focus on a different type of client.

Differentiation. Differentiation rides on the back of positioning, and declares how you're different from those who offer the same or similar services. Vision and mission help you separate from your direct competition by defining your competitive advantage.

Messaging. When you have vision and mission for your business it's easy to describe what you do, and what you don't do. This helps in your professional networking and marketing efforts. As an example, when I tell people I'm a designer, they often ask if I can help them choose color schemes for their home, or advise on how to remodel something. Because of my mission and vision, I can correct their thinking.

WHAT IS A VISION STATEMENT?

Vision is both inspirational and aspirational, and describes an ideal situation or future. It's less specific than a mission, and doesn't address the how, but the desired results of your efforts.

Vision statements generally consist of a single sentence and communicate the ideal destination or achievement to be pursued. They are directional and long-term. You shouldn't need to change your vision statement, but you can change your mission statement and still maintain the same vision.

A vision statement should be concise, to the point, future-focused, and inspiring. It should not be a how-to statement. It's a *why*, not a *what*, declaration. It doesn't deal with the how, but the desire. You can observe this in these examples of vision statements:

> *A world where education, culture, and science are equitably shared as a means to benefit humanity.*
> — Creative Commons

> *To connect the American family to the American farm, so that every person can know and trust where their meat comes from.*
> — Good Ranchers

> *Be the most preferred and trusted financial institution serving the military and their families.*
> — Navy Federal Credit Union

When you identify your vision you will gain clarity about your WHY and are more likely to stay motivated through the twists and turns of the freelance journey.

WHAT IS A MISSION STATEMENT?

Mission outlines how the vision is achieve. It's specific, practical, and guides day-to-day decisions in and for the business. Examples of mission statements:

> *We strive to be Earth's most customer-centric company, Earth's best employer, and Earth's safest place to work.*
> — Amazon

> *Walmart's mission is to help people save money so they can live better.*
> — Walmart

> *Teaching a million to reach a billion.*
> — Joseph Z Ministries

HOW TO USE VISION AND MISSION

Both mission and vision are road maps rather than marketing statements, although you might choose to publish them in some form on your website and in promotional materials. They are essential compasses for your marketing, branding, and decision-making.

My vision for my creative work is to *glorify God in the marketplace through excellence, wisdom, and skill, and to teach others to do the same.*

The mission of my design practice is reflected in the copy on my home page: *Blending strategic thinking with aesthetic intelligence to create exceptional solutions that accelerate your growth, connect with your audience, and increase your competitive advantage.* By including the phrases *strategic thinking* and *aesthetic intelligence,* I'm filtering out certain types of prospective clients — those who are looking for a commodity — and inviting those who will make an investment in their success.

Decisions about my business are made based on alignment with my vision and mission. For example, how I integrate AI tools in my business systems and creative process is guided by my vision, mission, and values. I place a high value on bespoke work. Because of it, I eschew the use of templates, pre-built website themes, and DIY platforms. I study historic movements, trends, and styles to build my visual vocabulary. Even my creative process reflects my vision in that I begin with the question of why and approach strategy using the Socratic method. If a method or purpose requires compromising my values, I will not incorporate it, even if it makes something more convenient.

To uncover your vision, return to your purpose or divine calling. Why do you want to create for a living? Why do you want to freelance? What do you want to achieve for yourself and be known for? To craft your mission, carefully consider who you want to work with, what type of work you want to do for them, and how you will provide value to them. Mission and vision will help you filter out undesirable projects, help you keep boundaries intact in working relationships, and create appropriate goals and objectives for your business and creative growth.

WHY WRITE IT DOWN?

Writing your purpose, vision, and mission are Biblical concepts. As I noted in the previous chapter, Habakkuk was instructed to write out the vision *so that he who reads may run with it.*

A principle that's stuck with me through the years might also be helpful for you: *Paper remembers it so that your brain doesn't have to.*

Writing something down — mission, goal, reminder, whatever — is an act of commitment and remembrance. As commitment, it is firmly established as something you can return to time and time again and be guided in daily decision-making. It calls to mind why you're taking certain risks. As a remembrance, it secures and solidifies your purpose, and you can recognize when you've achieved it.

PART 2

MINDSET

YOUR ESTABLISHED SET OF ATTITUDES

CHAPTER TEN

THE REALITIES OF FREELANCING

A comparison of perceptions and realities.

Freelancing can be compared to a great adventure in which you go from project to project following your dreams and pursuing your passions exactly as you want to. You have total freedom. You can work wherever and whenever you want to, whether from home and starting the day with coffee and journaling with your dog at your feet, at your local coffee shop in the afternoon, or on the road in your satellite-connected van conversion. There's a certain romance to being untethered, working for yourself, and being your own boss. These are very real rewards of working independently.

Every coin has two sides. On the flip side of this romantic vision we find the less desirable aspects of freelancing. Other than the obvious concern of not drawing a steady paycheck, there are things about freelancing, especially as a creative, that are truly inconvenient. We don't always encounter these until we've made the leap into independence, and then we're derailed. Even then the rewards of flexibility, freedom and self-determination will balance or exceed these difficulties, making the inconveniences more than worth it.

As with any inconvenience, we can address and adapt, or accept and work with it. The mindset shift is this: Consider the inconveniences as opportunities to fortify your business systems and policies. These are my top five inconveniences most freelancers experience:

1. You're on your own. While working solo might be an introvert's joy, we don't often consider how being on your own plays out day to day. You have no fall-back position. There is no one to cover for you. Your mistakes are all your own, and they're entirely your responsibility.

Creatives who love teamwork and collaboration — the extroverts among us — may find themselves feeling cut off, starved for the energy of human interaction. One way to address this inconvenience is to build a network of peers. Join a professional association. Participate in a mastermind group. Join a networking group. Meet together regularly with fellow creatives for mutual support.

Be sure to connect with freelance creatives who are farther down the road than you are. Anyone who's ahead of you on the freelance journey and is experiencing success can share their experiences and how they've solved problems similar to those you're facing.

Seek wise counsel for important decisions (wise being the operative word here.) That means you should look outside the freelance realm into business, entrepreneurship, and creativity. Consult scripture. Read books about business, calling, and entrepreneurship. Engage legal and financial pros. Work with a business coach. Articles, podcasts, and videos are also useful resources.

If you know someone who's built a successful business, invite them for coffee and ask a lot of questions about the inconveniences they encountered and how they overcame them.

2. You're self-determined. This might seem more like a positive than a negative aspect, but it has its demerits. You are entirely responsible for the actions you take, the goals you set, and how you manage your time and money. Being self-motived and self-disciplined is critical. This may be a problem for you if you're used to working under team leaders, art directors or managers telling you what to work on, when to work, and how to work. Moving directly from school into freelancing, or from employment into independence, is a significant and often stressful change. Solve this problem by taking a look at your life goals, personally and professionally. Write out your goals and give them a timeline.

Identify your values and write them down. Decide what kind of work you want to create, what types of enterprises need it, and who is willing to pay for it. This defines your client prospect pool.

Look at what successful freelancers do who serve the same markets you want to serve. Consider them as resources to learn from, not as your competition.

Being self-determined means, among other things, that you determine how your freelance business operates and who you serve with the work you create.

3. You have to earn respect as a legitimate business. This is a tough one, and it's not about clients respecting you as a professional peer. It's more about how you're regarded by banks, landlords, and credit card companies.

When you're self-employed, it is not always easy to acquire necessary funding for your business. You will need to do more to prove your worth and trustworthiness than if you are on salary. This is not insurmountable, but it does require you to be faithful to pay your bills and to be able to prove your faithfulness by providing requested documentation.

It also requires you to have a legal business structure in place: a DBA filing, an LLC or corporation, appropriate business licenses, separation of business and personal financial accounts, and a method of accounting and bookkeeping.

4. You have to stay current with rapidly-evolving technology and tools. To re-state the obvious, technologies are constantly changing. It's necessary, as part of your self-determination, to understand the times and seasons, and roll with them.

Continually build your skills. Recognizing when you need training, software updates, computer upgrades, new marketing and networking methods, new goals, is crucial to your long-term success as a freelancer.

Artificial intelligence, although it's been around for awhile, has now emerged full force. Businesses, marketers, and creators are looking at how to take advantage of the technology for your business systems and creative process.

It may be that you need to reposition from full-time client-based work into licensing and product development, or into content creation to diversify your income. The manner in which you market needs to evolve according to trends in social media algorithms, emerging technology, how your clients use their devices, and where they spend their time. Address these concerns by paying attention to what's going on in the world and in your professional field. Become a trend-watcher. Attentively observe and revise your business and marketing strategies. Become comfortable with change.

5. You'll spend more time taking care of business than actually creating. This is a fact. In order to reach prospective clients, manage projects and accomplish the creative work, take care of business. Without clients, you have no revenue to live on and no work to create. Most independent professionals will admit that they spend most of their time working on their business, including planning, marketing, communicating, bookkeeping, paying bills, invoicing, and such.

You also need to manage your money well. While freelance income may ebb and flow, bills, rent and utilities remain constant. This is a fact of life for independent contractors.

Help yourself out by out-sourcing some tasks, setting up systems, planning your schedule in advance, systematizing and delegating. If you are not able to engage the help of professional assistants, use AI and app-based options to lighten your load. Schedule blocks of interrupted time each week and each month (based on the task) to work on your business.

What can you automate with software and apps? Invoicing, time tracking (if you bill hourly), marketing and email communications are some tasks that can be easily automated.

Investigate tactics of time blocking and task batching your business and personal activities to make the most of your days. Identify which activities and events you can postpone or delete from your calendar to make room to work on your business. Eliminate things that distract or that eat up your time (how much time do you spend scrolling, gaming, or streaming that you can invest into your business?)

In my experience, freelancing is the most rewarding and creative way to earn a living. Yes, there are difficult aspects to it. To become successful, you have to be intentional and wise.

Manage your expectations and know the risks. Develop professional relationships. Steward your time, money, and creative energy effectively. Treat your freelancing like a business.

CHAPTER ELEVEN

TOOLS, TALENT, AND SKILL

Define yourself by your ability to create, not to use tools well.

In this chapter I'm taking a different tack to the topic of the value of our creative work. It's sparked by a memorable conversation I had with a designer who had been freelancing for about three years. It's memorable because it caused me to adjust my own thinking significantly as I attempted to help him sort things out.

The designer expressed concern over his pricing and how other designers with less technical knowledge were undercutting his rates and winning the projects he was vying for. He was primarily using an online freelance marketplace to find clients and relying on his software and coding skills as the criteria for judging his value to clients. He didn't want to work for minimal compensation, having invested substantial sums in education, software, and hardware.

We took a look at his skill set. He was more than capable in everything from page layout for print, full stack web design, motion graphics and image editing. These are all valuable skills and assets to possess, but they didn't set him apart from his competitors.

I asked him about his approach with prospective clients, and learned that he shared a lot of information about his capabilities and accomplishments, and how he made a lot of effort into staying up to date with technologies. Then I made a statement that apparently shocked him a bit: "A designer is a designer whether using a computer or pencil and paper." I was surprised that he was so surprised by my statement. This was a foreign concept for him.

TOOLS

The creative tools we use today became normalized in the graphic arts industries only in the latter third of the 20th Century. That's not that long ago. Steve Jobs introduced the Macintosh, the first personal computer with a graphical interface, in early 1984. By 1993 the Mac was the go-to tool for graphic artists and designers, replacing paste-up artists, hot wax, type galleys, photostats, pica poles, rubylith, and Rapidograph pens, all of which had been standard tools of the graphic arts trades for decades previously. The line of separation between graphic designer and graphic artist disappeared. As the personal computer made those tools and roles obsolete, those tools had made earlier tools and roles obsolete.

People have been designing and illustrating for millennia, and capturing photographs for more than two centuries. Tools change, but the reasons for using the tools — communication and problem-solving — remain constant.

Creatives should not define themselves by the depth and breadth of their technical knowledge but by their ability to design. To design is to plan and create order. It involved purpose, planning, intention, and problem-solving. It's not fine art, which is self-expression. Absolutely we must stay up with the current tools of our trades. Even so, we must acknowledge that our tools pertain to our production processes, not to our thinking and design decisions. They are the how, not the what.

A side note: In talking from a design point of view I'm not excluding photographers, illustrators or even copywriters. This pertains to you and your approach to your craft if you are one of these rather than a designer.

Our focus, as stated in Chapter Two and Chapter Five, should be on creating solutions to the business, branding, communications, and marketing problems (gaps) that clients experience. A creative is a problem-solver. That's the value of our work.

SKILL

We tend to think of skill as physical ability, as competence to perform, as dexterity. We separate it from thought and label it manual labor — the skilled trades, for example — because it's regarded as physical and not cerebral, and somehow physical is less worthy than cerebral. Skill relates to excellent craftsmanship and developed expertise. The word *skill* comes from the Nordic origin, *skil*, and the Dutch, *geschil*. Its definition centers on difference, to distinguish. Take a moment to pause and think about that.

For us, skill is proficiency. In Exodus 35:31–35 the Hebrew word for *skill*, anglicized as *chakam*, denotes a more profound and robust understanding that involves wisdom, craftiness, prudence, discernment, moral insight, artistry, and spiritual depth. This is what Solomon asked God for. This is how God anointed Bezalel and Oholiab. True skill involves wisdom. Wisdom is the foundation for mastery of any craft or creative pursuit.

TALENT

A different conversation took place between some design students and myself and involved an observation that one had more talent than they, and was therefore better at acing design assignments which meant it was easier for them to earn an A.

People posses different measures of talent. Talent tends to go hand in hand with desire, but not always. A person can desire an ability but not have a high degree of talent for it. What is talent, what's its purpose, and what's its value for us freelance creatives?

Talent is defined as a natural aptitude or skill. There are many talented dog trainers who make a very good living by training dogs and training people to train their dogs. If you ever observe me on walks with my dogs you understand quickly that I have minimum amounts of talent and skill in that area. While I desire to be better at it and have made some effort at becoming trained, I have not invested the time and effort required to bring my dog into a proper heel. When a person has desire but lacks natural aptitude, they have to increase their effort to build skill.

Talent is merely potential. It must be developed. I've observed many talented people who relied on their natural ability but neglected to channel and mold it into something useful. Without focus and discipline, talent is worthless. I believe this was part of what Jesus was referring to in his parable of the talents in MATTHEW 25:14–30. Talent is easily wasted. We can possess certain talents and even take pride in them, but unless we train them, they're worthless both to us and others. We're to take responsibility for the gifts within us and develop them in meaningful ways. This is advice for everyone. I've worked with too many highly talented students who were reluctant and even opposed to putting in the effort and discipline to build skill and work toward mastery. Some even resigned projects, opting for a failing grade instead of doing the difficult work.

We can't make a living from our talents. We must become skilled, competent, and master our craft so that our talents become valuable to others. Building skill and mastery requires mind, soul, and body working together.

When we compare skill, tools, and talent we realize none of the three is greater than another. All three are criteria for mastery of your creative craft so you can deliver value to your clients. Talent without skill, or tools alone, don't accomplish anything. When you provide solutions to your clients you stand out from your competitors who are positioning on their tools. Consider this proverb: *Do you see a man skillful in his work? He will stand before kings; he will not stand before obscure men.* — PROVERBS 22:29 ESV

QUALITIES OF A CREATIVE PROBLEM-SOLVER

Whether self-trained or formally trained, creatives must possess the ability to:

- Create and innovate;
- Research, gather information, evaluate and curate based on a stated purpose;
- Apply attentive observation and critical thinking;
- Explore, assess, and test a range of possible options;
- Answer the *what if* questions;
- Discover a client's needs and develop appropriate solutions;
- Apply sound design principles for visual appeal and to support function;
- Critique their own work.

Not one of these qualities requires knowledge of Photoshop, Procreate, Revit, or Midjourney. The creative practitioner successfully marries art (aesthetic) principles with functional requirements for specific purposes. Technical ability and talent fill a supporting, not a defining, role. The desire of the successful freelance creative isn't self-expression but helping others.

In conclusion, you can't make a living by relying on talent alone, or on technical skill alone. In the marketplace you'll have less competition if you position as a skilled *problem-solver.* Avoid competing on price and skill, and offer results and solutions as your competitive advantage.

My recommendation to the designer competing on skill was to re-think what made him valuable in the marketplace and to reposition his messaging. A designer as problem-solver is far more useful in the world than one who relies on technical ability or talent alone.

CHAPTER TWELVE

ON BEING AN OWNER

Make this crucial mindset shift.

When you freelance you are a business owner and responsible for the successes and failures of your enterprise. Honestly, it can go either way, depending on your mindset and resulting choices. And whether you jump into freelancing from school or from employment, at some point you'll come to the realization that you've taken on the responsibilities of *ownership.*

Owners function differently from employees. While employees can be all in with their employer's business, as long as they work for someone else they will never be an owner. Their stake in the enterprise is limited. They can easily quit. They can pass accountability to coworkers and managers with little consequence. As owners, freelancers have no one else to blame. They must act in the best interests of their business or they will not be in business very long.

To build a successful freelance business, the creative professional must do both the creative (the fun work) and the business (the obligatory work) well. Doing the right things for your business will support your creative work.

You will spend a greater percentage of your time doing business things than creating things, especially during the first few years in business. That's just the reality of it. If your business skills are weak, you need to strengthen them. You can have all the creative talent in the world but if you don't do business well, you can't make a living from it.

SIX OWNERSHIP PRINCIPLES YOU NEED TO KNOW

Successful business owners take care of things. They prioritize, systematize, communicate, perform customer service, market and promote, pay their bills, and maintain their books. They serve their customers or clients. They integrate their business and personal lives, and operate from a solid framework of systems and policies. They set goals. They plan. They stay motivated.

Owners take action. They don't sit around until they are told what to do. They commit to the long, hard work of building a successful business. Owners strategize, plan and follow through quickly. When they fail at something — and they do fail — they use it as an opportunity to learn.

Owners honor their commitments. That means they meet the deadlines they set. They pay their contractors. They follow through on what they promise, even in the small things like responding to email and answering questions. And the first commitment an owner makes is to herself.

Owners develop the discipline to prioritize the non-creative things because they know they won't be in business very long otherwise. They keep their books up to date. They create and abide by a spending plan. They invoice on time. They pay their taxes. They set the vision and mission for their businesses. Sometimes they need to sacrifice other things in order to drive their business forward.

Owners learn to say no. If something will not add to their business, they take it on, but they accept the projects and responsibilities that lead to better projects and more business. Be selective. You can't please everyone, nor live up to expectations that are not yours. Be willing to release clients and refer unsuitable prospects elsewhere.

Owners are visionary. As an owner, you have to look down the road and envision your preferred future. Where do you want to be? What goals do you want to accomplish? What clients do you want to be working with? What will it mean for you to be that far along with accomplishments under your belt. What will it mean for the people who depend on you?

Owners delegate. There are tasks in your freelance business that you need to be doing, and there are tasks that you should not be doing. It's the little things that will steal your time and keep you from doing the work where you add value to your clients and yourself. What can you hand off to others or automate with technology?

ARE YOU DOING YOUR MOST IMPORTANT WORK?

I have found this to be true: **In order to be successful, we need to be hopeful about the future and absolutely honest about where we are at the present moment.** You see, where we are is our starting point. The future is our destination. Each day we begin from where we left off the previous day and continue. If we don't have clarity on our destination, we drive aimlessly, wasting time and energy. We need goals in order to stay on the right roads. Otherwise, we just check off items on to-do lists but accomplish very little great work.

COMMON STRUGGLES OF OWNER-FREELANCERS

When it comes to business, freelancers can struggle with the concept of ownership and the responsibilities of managing workload, money, clients, projects, business development, and inconsistent cash flow. We seek the freedom to create our work our way, but find ourselves grappling with the dull realities of making a living.

It helps to remember why you chose to freelance and your reasons probably include freedom, flexibility, and doing what you love. Not everyone can do what you do creatively, but millions have built and sustained businesses. Becoming skilled at doing business is fairly easy compared to mastering your creative craft, and it becomes easier the longer you pursue it. The most difficult aspect for me was making that mindset shift from creative to owner of a creative business. Once I had renewed my mind in that regard and had repeatable, automated systems and frameworks in place, I was able to focus on creating my core work and serving my clients.

It also helps to ask for advice and help. First and foremost, if you're a believer, your primary source and guide is your Creator. Submit your plans to him so that he can establish them (PROVERBS 16:3). Pursue his wisdom and counsel. And then work with all your heart as if you're working for the Lord, which you are (COLOSSIANS 3.23) Keep in mind that he's the source of your creative bent — he designed you. So place your trust in him and do the work you need to do. Take responsibility for your part in the work and he'll handle the rest.

Second, and also vital, rely on the wisdom, experience, and advice of reliable people. Don't take advice from anyone who doesn't want you to succeed. We all have naysayers who question and will even ridicule our plans. Accept the counsel of people who are on your side, in your corner, and support what you do — those who have your highest good in mind. If you decide to invest in a paid mentor or business coach, be circumspect in who that is. You will want someone who's been freelancing for long enough to have proven experience and insight you can learn from.

Accept that fact that trial and error are inherent in any creative process and in building a business. You will fail at some things, but don't let that deter you. Try again. Try a different way. When you need it, get professional advice from attorneys, accountants, financial advisors and business coaches. Connect with fellow creatives in person or online to stay inspired and encouraged.

CHAPTER THIRTEEN

PASSION AND PROFIT

Serving people is at the heart of your business.

The common advice is: *Do what you love and the money will follow.* This is a great ideal, because no one wants to spend the majority of their waking hours working at something they don't enjoy. There's a flaw in this thinking however. Doing what you love is not always a viable option in the marketplace. Unless there's a *need* in the marketplace for what you love to do, you can't build a successful business.

Designers, illustrators, photographers, and writers set up shop to do what they love, but can find themselves without clients and the ability to make a living. I wish we could all automatically make a living doing what we love to do, because our passions would sustain us for years to come and we'd always be fulfilled in our work. We can't just set up shop and hope clients will come knocking on our doors. They knock on our doors out of necessity. Their needs make our creative work viable.

In a previous chapter I stated that you can't make a living from your talent. You can't make a living from your passion, either. There's a very practical aspect to succeeding in the marketplace and that is the need of the buyer. Let's take a look at three reasons for your creative business to exist:

First, there is your passion. Being passionate about your work is grounded in your purpose, your desire to accomplish things, and your pursuit of personal fulfillment. Passion is defined as the intense desire or enthusiasm to do something. It is the energy and motivation behind what you do. If you've ever done work you're not passionate about, you'll understand the difference quickly.

You can't be passionate about everything. You're wired to have specific interests, make unique connections, and create from your own experiences and knowledge. You're more likely to pursue excellence and master your craft when you're passionate about your work. Do you need to be passionate about building a business? Basically, yes. You at least need to maintain the desire and enthusiasm to be successful.

Second, there is the need. Is there a need in the marketplace for what you want to do that people are willing to pay for? Will your creative thinking and resulting work product solve problems and satisfy needs?

Third, why do you want to start a business? The answer to this question has to go beyond simply wanting to be independent; it has to involve possessing a measure of desire to become a *creativepreneur.* In so many ways it's easier to work for someone else. Being someone's employee is far less risky than freelancing. Once you decide to start your business, keep in mind that it's not a business until you treat it like a business. Until then it's only a hobby.

No matter how large or small a business is, it will generally assume one of two roles: either a *producer* of goods or services, or a *marketer.*

As a producer you're first going to create something or offer a service, and then figure out how to sell it. In contrast, a marketer looks at what is needed and how to sell it, and then builds the product or offers the service. The producer focuses on the product while the marketer focuses on the need. Take a moment to consider your thoughts on this and whether you need to shift your thinking.

ABC Network's reality show, *Shark Tank*, very clearly highlights the difference between a producer focus and a marketer focus. People pitch all sorts of product ideas, and with every pitch the Sharks ask, "Is there a market? Do people want this?" Products and services have to be needed in the marketplace. You can have great talent and exude passion for your work but if you don't take a marketing approach, it will be more difficult to succeed.

The basis for marketing is identifying a need, and then creating a product or service that meets that need. You need to look at the market first. In launching a freelance business, a first strategy should be to find out what the need is. You first have to determine if there is a high-level need for your product or service. If there is, jump on in and build your business and your customer base. If there's not, figure out what adjustments you should make to your service offering in order to make it marketable.

If you've done your research and concluded that your product or service is marketable, your next step is how to *differentiate*. You are not the only creative professional in your field. There are many designers, writers, photographers, and illustrators in the world. It is crucial for you to understand that, in the marketplace, it's the *client* who has the power of choice. Why should they choose to work with you instead of Glenda's Amazing Design Services across the street? If you can position on something other than price, you can gain influence over the buying choices of your prospective clients. If you don't differentiate, you'll be regarded as just another creative services provider among myriad creative service agencies, and what you have to offer is just another commodity to be bought and sold based on cost.

SOME DEFINITIONS

Profession is a *paid* occupation, especially one that involves targeted training and a qualification (licensing, certification, etc.) process. It's assumed that professionals possess knowledge and expertise.

Vocation is defined as a strong feeling of suitability for a particular career or occupation. One has a job but pursues a vocation.

Passion, is an intense desire or enthusiasm for something. Passion is not a guarantee of success or satisfaction. In order to accomplish anything it must be partnered with practical, intentional effort.

Mission is a strongly felt aim, ambition, or calling.

We can conclude that when all four of these are merged the result is a strong conviction that motivates and directs our actions.

AN ABSOLUTELY NECESSARY MINDSET SHIFT

The purpose of establishing a business is to follow your passion. It should be to make money to meet your needs so that you can follow your passion. If your passion and your livelihood are the same, you are blessed and uncommon. Most of us who've been in business for any length of time have had to readjust, reinvent, and restart in order to maintain passion and profitability.

I didn't start out as a designer. I started out as an illustrator but quickly discovered that the market was not favorable to my original goals unless I was willing to relocate but it was favorable to design. So I adjusted. I changed my strategy and my customer base, and built my skills and reputation as a graphic designer. A few years later, I added web and digital design to my creative services. I shifted into brand strategy design. More recently, I started talking with emerging designers, students, and those wanting to make career changes, about how to freelance, and founded Freelance Road Trip.

Has my passion changed? No. But my business has. It's been more than forty years since I launched. At this point in my career I'm able to be selective about the projects and the clients I serve. I'm taking steps to add more passive income streams. My business is healthy. I am healthy, and my greatest work is ahead of me.

Being passionate about what you do for living or, in other words, making a living doing what you love, is useful if you can leverage that passion in the marketplace. If you can't, and you still want to build a freelance business, find out what you can leverage in the marketplace, and pursue your passion on the side. Sometimes it's simply a matter of tweaking your focus.

Successful freelancers not only find a niche but fulfill a need in the marketplace. Meeting a need is the purpose of any business. When we're able to make a living doing what we love, we're twice blessed. When you set up a business, you need to be profit-focused (the IRS will tell you that). In order to be profit-focused you need to be market-focused in that, if you don't go into business, what will the marketplace be missing?

CREATIVE BUSINESS

It's ideal that your life's work aligns with your reason for being (divine calling.) When your decisions and actions stem from your purpose, you are content, integrated, and unconflicted. Everyone has an intersection of how they're wired, what they enjoy doing, and how that work benefits others. But not everyone finds this intersection point.

It's a fact that many pursue their life work separately, as a side hustle or hobby, from how they make their living. Because of that, they often do not step into their purpose until retirement because of the time and energy demands of their jobs. But consider the potential impact when your purpose (what you're wired to do) and your profession (what you're paid to do) are in agreement. This is the preferred state of things, in my estimation, for supporting yourself and your household.

If you're entrepreneurial and a creative you must become skilled in doing business. There's no other option. If you don't enjoy doing business, think of it as a process and structure necessary to make a living from your work. Doing business effectively supports your creative work for clients, your personal creative projects, and underwrites your whole life.

How are you wired? What motivates you? What interests you? What do you enjoy doing? How will you transform what you enjoy doing into serving others? These are questions that every creative should be able to answer, and are the basis for your if you desire to earn a living and be satisfied from your creative work.

CHAPTER FOURTEEN

PROFIT MOTIVE

You're supposed to make money.

Profit motive is the intention to make a profit. *Motive* is the reason behind one's actions. *Profit* is financial gain. If you're in business, it is assumed you intend to make a profit. If you are a freelance creative, profit motive is a requirement. Otherwise, it's a hobby.

As a freelance creative, the question whether you're running a business or enjoying a hobby can be a concern. Art, design and photography are also types of hobbies pursued for fun and personal satisfaction rather than profit. In fact, there are clients who prefer that we perform our work for the love of it alone and not care about being paid. But we have the right to profit from our talents and skills, and if we choose to do so, we need to go about it correctly so that we can earn a living.

DEMONSTRATE A PROFIT MOTIVE

If you have a profit motive, you must show *intent* to make a profit. This does not mean you must make a profit every year in order to claim deductible expenses on your tax filings, but if you're not profitable, what are you doing? It is for this reason that I admonish you to be business-minded, put necessary legal frameworks into place, and to promote your work to a well-defined target audience of prospective clients. The frameworks help to protect your livelihood from *hobby-loss* designation in case of a tax audit.

These are some ways that demonstrate you are intentionally and seriously running a business and pursuing profitability:

√ Invest time regularly and consistently in business activities.

√ Create a written business plan.

√ Create a written marketing plan.

√ Set up business checking, savings and credit lines, separate from your personal accounts.

√ Obtain a business license with your city or county.

√ File a DBA (Doing Business As or Fictitious Business Statement) usually with your county.

√ Obtain an EIN (Employer Identification Number) from the IRS.

√ Invest time and effort in business development through professional networking.

√ Form an LLC or S-corp.

√ Join your local chamber of commerce.

√ Pay self-employment taxes.

√ Obtain a resale license and collect and remit sales taxes on tangible goods sold.

√ Set up accounting or bookkeeping software and create income and expense categories that relate to the Schedule C.

√ Invest financially in self-promotion and marketing activities.

√ Charge for your creative services.

√ Use written contracts.

√ Register your copyrights.

√ Create and maintain a website for your business.

If you like to create things and occasionally sell something, you are more likely a *hobbyist*. Hobbyists may be able to deduct certain expenses, but only to the limit of what they earn from their hobby. If a hobbyist earns $300 in a year they can deduct only up to $300 of hobby-related expenses. You cannot claim a loss from a hobby.

If you intend to profit from your creative work, you have to engage in business activities. Freelance creatives serve clients, which is a different profit-making activity than creating work to sell. By freelancing you're demonstrating your intent to make a profit.

PROFIT INTENT VS. ACTUALITY

Profit motive involves more than making a profit from your business efforts. The Internal Revenue Service (IRS) understands that there is a difference between profit *motive* and profit *actuality*. The IRS looks at *everything* you do for your business, not just at profit and loss. It can take several years for a self-employed independent creative to realize a profit. Per the Hobby Loss Rule, three profitable years out of five indicates there is a profit motive. If your business isn't profitable it may be considered a hobby and your expense deductions will be limited. You need to remain in profit motive mode. This is especially true if you are freelancing part time while also employed in a W2-based role at a company you don't own.

If you are carrying on your work with the intent of making a living or adding to your income — i.e., you are engaged in trade or business — you can *demonstrate a profit motive* even if you show a loss in a given year, or for a couple years in a row.

The IRS checklist for establishing a profit motive includes these nine criteria:

1. How you run your business. Are you focusing on making money? Are you keeping records? Do you invoice? Are you licensed? Are you doing what business owners do?

2. Do you have the necessary skills? Expertise is not only about being amazing at your creative work, but about being an amazing business owner. Are you actively engaged in learning how to run your business? Hobbyists generally do not earn degrees or certificates in their hobby. If you have studied and matriculated, or earned a certificate in the area of your freelance work, or taking courses, that shows motive for earning a living as a professional.

3. How much time do you spend regularly and actively engaged in working on your business? If you freelance as a side gig while being a full-time or part-time employee, the time you spend may be significant in determining if you are in business or doing a hobby.

4. How likely are you to profit in the future? If you build your business to be able to sell it in the future, would you profit from the sale? Freelancers don't have a lot of assets compared to small business owners with a shop, employees, and equipment. What are you doing now, where are you investing time and money, to ensure revenue over the long term? Photographers can sell and license their photos, illustrators can sell prints, paintings, and drawings, and designers can sell their designs. The more revenue channels you develop (selling prints, licensing images, selling templates, etc.) the more likely it is that you can create consistent revenue streams.

5. Past related success. Have you owned or do you own other businesses that have turned profits? Are others making a living by doing what you're doing?

6. History of profit and loss. If you've been freelancing for some time and have shown a profit consistently in the past, a few bad years will not necessarily relegate you to hobby mode. If you are just starting out, you need to build, gain momentum and put systems in place to be able to turn a profit as early as possible.

7. Occasional profits. Freelance income ebbs and flows. If you earn a substantial creative fee on a single project, that occasional profit may be substantial enough to show profit motive. Having one or two high-revenue projects can offset the rest of the year when you're not earning as much.

8. Is freelancing your only source of income? If so, you are considered to be in profit motive mode. If you freelance part time while employed, you cannot rely on this criterion alone.

9. Personal pleasure. If your business is not generally considered a source of personal pleasure or recreation, the IRS can easily consider you to be in business to make a profit. Self-employed creative independents engaged in illustration, photography or design do what they do because they both enjoy it and want to earn their living by it, even though these disciplines are also common hobby pursuits.

You don't need to meet all nine criteria in order to prove you're engaged in business, but you should establish your profit motive on as many of them as possible. Remember, **it's not a business until you treat it like a business.**

Given the current landscape and the myriad opportunities for freelancers to thrive, there is reduced potential that you will be considered a hobbyist for income tax purposes. Even so, take the nine points from the IRS, take a look at your freelance business, determine where you need to make some *profit motive* changes, and make those changes. It's also highly recommended to discuss your business with an accountant or tax attorney.

CHAPTER FIFTEEN

FREELANCE OR FOR HIRE?

Clarifying the working relationship.

Misunderstandings can exist between clients and freelance creatives regarding their working relationships. Questions such as owns the working files, what files are provided to the client, when and how the project gets accomplished can cause stress for both parties if left unanswered. I have worked with clients who attempted to treat me as their employee and can attest first-hand to the tension that results.

Both parties come into the working relationship with assumptions and expectations. For the client and the freelancer alike, proper classification of their roles and contractual relationship will help them avoid tax liabilities and potential penalties for *misclassification* of worker status. Basically, there are two forms of contracted relationships. Below I discuss these from a designer's point of view but they pertain to creatives in general.

THE EMPLOYEE

If you're a staff or in-house designer, you are an employee, and you are automatically in a work-for-hire, also called work-made-for-hire, relationship with your employer. Everything you create under a scope of work belongs to your employer including preliminary work, native files, and rights of use. Your employer is the legal author of the work and controls it. Whether or not you may use the work in your own portfolio depends upon your employer's policies.

Employers determine when, where and how their employees work, how they will be paid, what benefits they receive, and pays their salaries. They remit payroll taxes on behalf of their employees and deduct the taxes from paychecks. Employers also supervise and train their employees, provide tools, equipment and materials, determine vacation schedules, PTO, and other benefits, and decide what an employee is paid. Employees can quit and employers can fire. Employees receive a W2 earnings statement from the employer for tax filing purposes.

Freelancers who obtain clients through *talent agencies* are employees of the agency for the duration of the engagement. The agency takes taxes and other deductions from the salaries and remits them to the government and provides a W2 wage statement for income tax reporting.

THE INDEPENDENT CONTRACTOR

Freelancers are *independent contractors* and are therefore self-employed. They work on a per-project basis; control the rights to their work; determine when, where and how they work; work with multiple clients concurrently; choose who they work with; provide their own equipment, work space, materials, and training, invoice for the work performed, and are responsible for paying their own taxes. They invest in their businesses, engage in marketing and promoting their work; can sub-contract aspects of a project; and cannot be dismissed by their clients except as contracted. Independent contractors can't resign a project without fulfilling their contracted obligations to the client. They may receive a 1099 statement of earnings from the client for tax filing purposes, depending on the payment method used to pay invoices.

Independent contractors are the authors of the work they create, whether done for a client or as a personal project. As the author of the work, the independent contractor negotiates the sale or licensing of usage rights to the client. The client receives what is agreed upon, and the freelancer is able to include the work in their portfolios and promotions, and reserves all other rights for themselves. They may license the same work to different parties, depending on what their contracts state.

WORK-FOR-HIRE AND THE INDEPENDENT CONTRACTOR

If a freelancer agrees to a work-for-hire relationship with a client, they're basically making themselves employees without receiving the benefits of employment. Organizations such as the Graphic Artists Guild have advocated against work-for-hire contracts for freelancers because the freelancer gives up all rights to and control of the work they create under these contracts. But it remains up to the individual freelancer whether or not to accept work-for-hire contracts. This is part of the freedom of being independent.

If you're a freelancer in the United States, work-for-hire *must be agreed upon in writing in advance of doing the work*, and the work being done must meet certain IRS and United States Copyright Office criteria.* It must be created as part of:

(1) a translation,

(2) a contribution to a motion picture or other audiovisual work,

(3) a contribution to a collective work (such as a magazine),

* https://www.copyright.gov/circs/circ30.pdf

(4) as an atlas,

(5) as a compilation,

(6) as an instructional text,

(7) as a test,

(8) as answer material for a test,

(9) or a supplementary work (i.e., "a secondary adjunct to a work by another author" such as a foreword, afterword, chart, illustration, editorial note, bibliography, appendix and index).

The work-for-hire model becomes problematic when applied to independent contractors, because we make a living via our portfolios and need to be able to promote and display our work without restriction. Many designers (myself included) avoid work-for-hire contracts by licensing rights instead.

Clients who require work-for-hire contracts need to be sure they have written agreements with the freelancer, and that these contracts are signed *prior* to the start of the project. Clients should also realize that they're *contracting* freelancers, not *hiring* them as employees.

Be aware that certain industries, including publishing, media, entertainment, and others in which the client needs to own the IP (intellectual property) require work-for-hire engagements.

GRAY AREAS

There are always gray areas. For example, a freelancer who works on site at a business under the supervision of the business for the duration of a project or a limited period of time is very likely to be considered an employee under California's AB5[†] law and the Independent Contractor Rule[‡] implemented in March 2024 by the National Labor Relations Board (NLRB). If a freelance photographer contracts a freelance retoucher, the retoucher may be deemed an

† https://www.ftb.ca.gov/file/business/industries/worker-classification-and-ab-5-faq.html

‡ https://www.dol.gov/agencies/whd/fact-sheets/13-flsa-employment-relationship

employee and the photographer becomes responsible as an employer. These are the NLRB criteria to determine if the independent contractor is an employee of the client or in business for himself:

√ Opportunity for profit or loss depending on managerial skill,
√ Investments made by the worker and the employer,
√ Permanence of the working relationship,
√ Nature and degree of control,
√ Whether the work performed is integral to the client's business, and
√ Skill and initiative.

It's necessary for freelance creatives to stay abreast of current and proposed labor laws in their state and nationally, to avoid potential misclassification under Department of Labor policy. The burden of whether a worker is dependent on the client or is in business for himself is placed by the government on the client and not the freelancer. We who desire to be independent contractors should be able to freely choose for ourselves how we should be classified. As such, we need to demonstrate in fact that we're owners of our own businesses and not reliant on clients to control and direct our work.

As an independent designer and illustrator, I don't assume that my clients know what our working relationship is. My contracts specifically state that our relationship is not a work-for-hire. I also specify what rights are transferred to the client, and when. Including these clauses has prevented misunderstandings and wrong assumptions. Disagreements over who owns what, and what the client actually pays for and receives, are avoided. Additionally, I'm careful to discuss the *project* rather than the *job*, and to use phrases such as "working *with*" rather than "working *for*."

MANAGE EXPECTATIONS

I cannot over-emphasize the necessity of understanding your working relationship with your clients. Avoid assumptions, presumptions, confusion, and manage expectations on your part and that of your client by clearly defining the working relationship in writing through your contract, and require your clients to sign your contracts before you begin the work.

Additionally, know what's going on with labor laws and legislation both nationally and in your state. Become your own activist and advocate for your right to work as a freelancer, unencumbered by employee-employer requirements. It's simple and quick to write your legislators and post to or message them on social media. Don't neglect this aspect of business ownership. Legislation impacts not only your business but the entire freelance community.

CHAPTER SIXTEEN

TWELVE RULES FOR SUCCESS

Implementing wise restraints that make us free.

Rules are useful tools to keep oneself in check, to maintain boundaries and to avoid issues. Rules are expressed or privately-held regulations or principles that govern conduct in a specified activity or area of knowledge. Every person and enterprise runs on rules. We have rules of the road that keep us safe on the highway, rules of etiquette, and rules for the games we play. I've found that the more experienced we become in life and in business, the more rules we have.

I want to share a few of my rules which have helped me stay in business for decades and which have kept me from making a lot of bad decisions. Some have been formed on the fly and others have been established as the result of my own ignorance and mistakes.

Some are simply common sense. No matter what the impetus is for creating a rule, its overall purpose is to *protect* my creativity and livelihood.

MY 12 RULES FOR FREELANCE SUCCESS

Rule No. 1. **Don't accept projects that contradict your values.** If you are uncomfortable with the premise of the project or the goals of the client, pass it by. It's not worth it to take on a creative project just for the money and end up hating the work. Invariably, no amount of money will make up for compromising your personal or professional standards.

Rule No. 2. Don't accept a new client if there's even the hint of trouble ahead. Trouble comes in many forms and will always sap your joy and creative energy. No working relationship is perfectly smooth, but some are downright not worth it. The trouble is usually not about the project itself but about how you and the client interact. When a client wants to tell you how you should do the work, when they seem to not know what they want, when they fish for ideas or want you to do spec work before they will commit to the project, when they are secretive about their project... when they think actually hiring instead of contracting you... these are all red flags.

Rule No. 3. Apply critical thinking. Computers, software, and AI are tools. No software can provide the wisdom, knowledge, and skill required to create — these attributes are God-endowed. Personal computers have existed since the mid-1980s. Designers and artists have been creating for millennia.

Rule No. 4. Take a day off every week. Just as you need to exit the road to re-fuel or re-charge your car, you need to take a break regularly. Most of the freelancers I know work long hours, including weekends. An annual two-week vacation is not enough to regroup and sustain ongoing productivity. Stopping work to rest and reflect every week — taking a sabbath/sabbatical — is essential for long-term success, good health, and satisfaction. Unplug, slow down, and reflect on what you're doing and why. You're able to put things in perspective when you step outside the flow of daily creative effort.

I admit to struggling with the concept of weekly rest or sabbath. While many think of a sabbath in religious terms, and consider it to be boring, restricting, even legalistic, experience has taught me that time off and time apart allows me to reboot, and gives me perspective from a different point of view — in my case, from God's point of view. My struggle is often with the mindset that rest — not working — isn't productive, and it's even a waste of time. For me, rest means:

- *Slowing* my pace.
- Doing the work of *life maintenance*: cleaning, cooking, gardening; and *self-maintenance*: reading, hiking, spending time with family and friends, planning, study, reflection, prayer.
- Reviewing my WHY and divine calling, and assessing where I need to adjust and make course corrections.

Rule No. 5. Design your days. The design process includes planning and being purposeful, knowing where you need to end up before you begin. This applies to managing your own time in order to be effective in your work. If you plan each day before you begin it, you'll keep distractions to a minimum and are more likely to stay focused. At minimum, plan each week ahead of time, leaving room in it for the unexpected. Plan things out first thing in the morning or the night before, you have a road map to follow that will keep you on course.

Rule No. 6. Always be observant. Keep your eyes open. Everything is potential inspiration. I teach my students about *attentive observation*, which is the *practice* of looking at and evaluating something in order to understand it better. I am always looking for inspiration, and often find it in sources that are entirely unrelated to the projects I'm working on.

Rule No. 7. Always be listening. Not many people take the time to develop listening skills, but doing so can put your ahead of your competitors. Clients are more likely to trust someone who listens and then applies what they've heard. Listen for what problems you can solve. Most creative work done for clients meets a need or solves a problem. Listen for what's not being said directly but implied.

Rule No. 8. Don't edit when brainstorming. The best creative solutions are known to come from "brain dumps" where you just start listing and/or doodling everything that comes to mind in pursuit of a design solution. Once a list is made, review it and narrow it down. Creating a mind map — a loose, non-linear, hierarchical chart that brings an idea front and center and uses lines (pathways) to make connections to related ideas. that helps you to make associations you didn't recognize before.

Rule No. 9. Do not work-for-hire or on spec. I discussed work-for-hire in the previous chapter. It, along with speculative work which includes certain types of contests, devalues your work and your contribution to the client's success. They also deprecate the design profession as a whole.

Rule No. 10. Always begin a project with a handshake AND a written contract AND a down payment. The handshake helps establish the relationship with the client. The contract protects the relationship by outlining specific expectations that both parties have agreed to. Most designers I know will concur on this: It's when you don't have a written agreement that trouble shows up. The down payment establishes trust in the working relationship, and sustains you while you work.

Rule No. 11. The client is not your enemy. The freelancer-client relationship should be one of mutual respect. The freelancer is there to serve the client. The client is there to facilitate the freelancer. It's a give-give relationship. When disagreements arise or a mistake is made, own your part in it, fix it, and continue. Don't blame. I've known too many designers (and even have been guilty of it myself on occasion) who complain about their client constantly. And I've worked with clients who complain about their previous designers. Both freelancer and client should be about the business of seeking the other's highest good.

Rule No. 12. Practice gratitude which helps us stay humble. Our work relies on providence and the good will of our clients, family, and friends. Thank your clients for the projects they send your way. Show your appreciation and you'll be appreciated. The other aspect of being thankful is to the Creator. Your clients are part of his providence. Never forget that it's God who gives us the ability to create wealth.* That's part of his covenant with us.

RULES ABOUT MAKING RULES

One rule to rule everything else: **Determine what your values and non-negotiables are before you engage with clients.** Setting boundaries yourself inhibits others from setting them for you. When you decide in advance about how you will handle a situation it makes it easier to respond appropriately when the situation occurs. Setting and maintaining boundaries will help you avoid relationships and circumstances that are potentially harmful to you and your business.

Be consistent in upholding your values, but also be flexible. There are times when times you will need to add, relax, or modify a rule.

Take some time this week to make a list of your own rules. These are not your values but may be based on them. Your rules become your business policies, and are more about how you operate your freelance business tactically.

For example, a value may be to separate work time from personal or family time. The rule might then be about maintaining set working hours, or going offline and shutting your studio door to focus on your family during weekends.

* "And you shall remember the LORD your God, for it is He who gives you power to get wealth, that He may establish His covenant which He swore to your fathers, as it is this day."
– DEUTERONOMY 8:18 NKJV

CHAPTER SEVENTEEN

IDLING AND ACCELERATION

Taking action makes you ready.

"I'll get to it when I'm ready."

I'm sure you've had the experience of planning to get something done and then postponing until it became absolutely necessary to do it. This tendency is referred to as *procrastination*, which is the action of putting off something until tomorrow. The root is Latin, *procrastinat*, meaning *to forward to tomorrow*. Or, not getting around to it at all. I've operated that way a lot in my past, and still struggle with it from time to time. My students often procrastinate, claiming it's their preferred way to operate because somehow they're more creative under pressure. Maybe so.

I've learned from experience that procrastination can be a mistake, especially when you don't know what's coming. Taking control now prepares you for what you will encounter on the road ahead.

We can't run our businesses solely on spur-of-the-moment actions and last-ditch efforts. Although we tend to put off doing things until we feel we're ready, what we don't understand is that **it's in taking action and moving forward that we become ready**. We make ourselves ready by taking action.

Back when I coached girls softball, I wanted to instill in each player the confidence to take charge of the ball whether they were hitting, catching or throwing. I talked about gripping the ball. I demonstrated how to hit, how to throw and how to field. I showed them how to reach out for the ball with their glove and grab it rather than waiting for it to land in the pocket. It was not until each player began to hit, catch and throw that they faced their fear of the ball, built skill and realized they could affect the outcome of a game. With each small success, they traded their fear for confidence.

Our default as humans is to wait until we have the confidence to do something, not realizing that it's in the doing that confidence is built. So if we wait until we're ready, we never will be. We must make ourselves ready.

DON'T WAIT TO BECOME READY

To use driving as an analogy, we can spend time idling at the intersection, anticipating the exact optimum moment to move forward. We wait for the traffic light to turn green. Then we accelerate quickly to full speed. Then we come to the next intersection and slow down, come to a stop, and idle once again.

Idling is when the engine is running but we're not moving. It a state of *potential* motion. Over the years I've spent way too much time idling, anticipating taking action but not getting around to it.

I prefer the open road. A vehicle that moves at a steady pace uses fuel more efficiently than one that slows, idles, and accelerates over and over again. To realize success as independent creatives, we need to move forward consistently, even if we do it slowly, and even when we think we're not yet ready. When we make the commitment to move and step out, that's when we begin building competence, and from that, confidence.

THE FOUR CS OF BUILDING MOMENTUM

Courage is defined as *strength in the face of fear, the ability to do something that's frightening.* The word has a Latin root, *cor,* meaning heart.

Often we delay moving forward out of fear. Or we're uncertain of the outcome. Deciding to move forward without knowing if you will be successful takes courage. There is no "safe place" for the courageous. They step out into the unknown and take on the challenge. If they fail, they shake it off and step out again.

When you procrastinate, you're not taking charge of your success. You're allowing distractions and current circumstances to determine your actions and keep you from the activities necessary to build and sustain your business. You also put yourself in danger of not having enough time and resources later on. Really, what are you waiting for? Is your reason for waiting realistic?

Commitment dedication to something. *Deciding* to do something is not doing it. There's anecdote about four birds sitting on a wire, and one decided to fly away. How many are left? Four. Because the bird only decided to fly away. You can decide to do something and still not do it. You have to take action on it. Once you decide to move forward, take a step, then take the next step, and commit to taking next steps after that. Successful careers are built one step at a time.

One way I've learned to commit is to know what my motives are. Why is a goal or action necessary? What will I get out of it? What's the benefit? What if I do nothing? Setting a goal for no reason will usually result in not achieving the goal. Keep the reason for the goal in mind. Understand that inaction has as much consequence as action and is motivation enough for most people to get moving.

Competence is defined as *the ability to do something successfully.* When you do a thing for the first time, it's easier to do it again, especially if you're successful. The more you do something, the better you get at doing it.

If I reach out to one new prospect and gain them as a regular contact, that's a win, and I am more capable of reaching out the next time. I become better at it and increasingly successful at building connections more often. If I am able to convert that contact into a client, I become more capable in conversion. Repetition creates success. As you act on things, you get used to the progress you make, and you're less likely to put things off so often.

Confidence is *firm trust, belief, reliance on or in something*. The more often you do something, the more adept you become at it. Increased skill leads to increased confidence. Confidence is a direct outgrowth of capability. As your confidence grows, your fear subsides. You become sure of yourself.

These four companions — courage, commitment, competence, and confidence — work together for anything you do creatively in business and personally. When you get through one full cycle from courage to confidence the next daunting task or goal is less intimidating because you've been successful in the past and you will be successful again in the future. You've solved problems and prevailed over challenges in the past, and you will overcome them in the future. While we don't rest on past successes, they encourage us to keep moving forward.

To achieve anything requires action. Is there a great idea you know you need to take action on but haven't yet? Is someone else waiting on you to get going? What have you been postponing or procrastinating on? What else becomes possible once you've accomplished it?

Take a moment to write down something you've been idling on. Consider why you've been putting it off.

Then, list 3 sequential actions steps you will take. Include when you will accomplish each — give each a due date — and add them to your calendar. Then, follow through on each date.

Refuse to idle. Make the commitment. Move before you think you're ready. You're probably more ready than you think you are.

CHAPTER EIGHTEEN

THE ART OF BALANCE

A proportional approach to balancing your life

Your creative business runs on goals, schedules, policies, and systems. It's important to design your time, implement policies, and set up systems in your business, but also in the personal parts of your life, so that everything runs smoothly.

The accepted principle in our culture is known as *work-life balance* which is understood to be an equilibrium between professional life and personal life. It proposes that there are two are separate aspects of one's life that must be equalized. Work intersects and is impacted by one's personal life, and vice versa. The understood ideal is that work time and personal time are symmetrically balanced in a 50:50 ratio. If a mother takes a personal day to take care of a sick child, her job is impacted. When a deadline looms and overtime is required it impacts the man who will miss his nephew's soccer match because of it. These two scenarios alone prove that work time and personal time are merged. They each bear on each other.

Corporations and institutions train their employees in work-life balance with an aim to increase productivity through managing one's time. Programs and policies are implemented which allow parental leave, flex time, sabbaticals, and remote work. Of all the resources available to us, time is the only one that everyone has the same amount of. Once a minute has passed, it's gone. We cannot reclaim, recycle or renew it. The difference between achieving our dreams and goals or not is mostly based on how we use our time resource. It's fairly easy to be efficient, but being effective in our use of time is often a crap shoot.

Myriad books, blogs and influencers attempt to solve problems of time management and productivity. Bullet journaling, decorative and functional planning, calendars, agendas, and apps are popular choices for managing (I actually prefer the word, stewarding) time.

Freelance creatives juggle many concurrent tasks and projects, each at a different stage of development and complexity. Incoming client requests, unplanned events, and personal obligations compete for our attention while we're trying to get a project out the door. We experience a constant tension between the task at hand and the one waiting to be started. While I'm working on one project I'm feeling the pressure of another. Does this sound familiar to you?

When you're building a freelance business, especially when you work from home, professional and personal time tend to merge. While a few freelancers I know attempt to maintain a 40-hour work week and take evenings and weekends off, the greater portion live and work fluidly: everything kind of blends together.

When my daughter was young I was able to take off a couple afternoons every week to be at her games. I even coached her softball team for several years. I often took my dogs on midweek hikes because the trails were less crowded than on weekends.

My schedule follows a pattern with a great deal of flexibility built in. I begin the day with coffee, Bible study, journaling, prayer, and planning. Then I start my workday. I walk my dogs and then go back to work until about mid-afternoon when I run errands. In the evening I take the dogs on another walk, then eat dinner, and return to work for a few hours. When there are client meetings, appointments, or something else comes up, I adjust my routine. For me the flexibility of my schedule is one thing I dearly love about freelancing.

WORK-LIFE INTEGRATE.

The thing I've come to understand is that life is a whole, a *gestalt*, and made up of different parts or roles. Symmetry — the typical idea of work–life balance — is not the goal when managing time. When building a business, you're naturally going to spend more time on your business, which gives you less time for personal pursuits. When your business is established and you're maintaining it you will be spending more or less time in it and on it depending on what else is going on in your life. Freelancing gives you freedom and flexibility, but you must manage it.

ESTABLISH GUARDRAILS

Guardrails are protective barriers strategically placed to protect areas of high risk. As self-employed persons we can easily become distracted or compromised during our workdays by interruptions and unexpected events. As such, it's necessary to install conceptual fences and barriers that protect our creative energy and focus. We also need to place boundaries around precious personal time, such as being with our family. Some of my guardrails include:

- Don't respond to client texts, calls, or emails on weekends or weekday evenings.
- Send all incoming calls to voicemail unless they're from specific people in my contact list.
- Systematize and automate email so that incoming messages are automatically routed into specified folders. Set up filtering

parameters for junk and scam email so that they're automatically routed to the trash bin.

- Schedule client meetings or run errands after noon to protect my peak creative time which is in the morning.
- Observe a sabbath (a day off) every week to rest, recreate, reflect, and remember the Creator while enjoying his creation.

Set boundaries and enforce them. Managing time, which is our most precious resource, is vital to accomplishing significant things. The primary tactics for guarding our time is to remove distractions and reduce interruptions. Distractions are usually small, and we don't notice we're being pulled off course because most of them are in some way necessary. Some of my distractions have been my inbox, phone calls, text messages, and scrolling.

While distractions are things you directly control, interruptions come at you externally. People and circumstances will demand your attention and pull you away from your work. One method of dealing with this is to schedule blocks of time in which you don't respond to requests, or allow any communication at all. As an example, a pastor friend of mine designates Wednesdays for study and research, and is unavailable for any contact the entire work day. He burrows in and get things accomplished without interruption. Cal Newport discusses this "hermit" strategy in his book, *Deep Work*.

Setting boundaries requires enforcement. Boundaries are only as strong as you make them. People and events will rob your time if you allow them to. Setting and maintaining guardrails allows for flexibility and spontaneity while still protecting what you want to protect. Every wall has a gate in it somewhere. The key is to know when to open it or keep it shut.

Identify your distractions and determine how you'll manage them. People and tasks both can be distracting time-suckers. One of my distractions has been scrolling. I'll admit to having wasted so much time on something that has little value in my life. Time is wasted when we do the wrong thing at the wrong time.

DESIGN YOUR DAYS

It's easier to keep your time boundaries and well-being intact if you plan things out. Planning ahead enables you to move through your days with intention. These are things to guide you in setting your guardrails, and are extremely helpful if you work from home.

1. **Design your week ahead of time.** Take part of the Friday, Saturday, Sunday prior to assess the week being completed and plan the week ahead, schedule appointments, projects, and tasks. Include your personal and professional time in this, because your life is made up of more than work. Scheduling an entire week rather than one day at a time allows you to effectively prioritize responsibilities.

2. **Block your time.** Time blocking is similar to the concept of watches in marine and military sectors. Divide each day into blocks: morning, afternoon, evening, night. These are each a block of time. They don't all need to be of the same duration. Set aside mornings for one type of activity, afternoons for another, evenings for a third, and sleep will usually happen during the remaining block.

   Be mindful of your circadian rhythms (the cyclical rise and fall of your energy). Energy levels and the ability to stay focused ebb and flow throughout the day. Most people have a consistent rhythm of energy peaks and troughs. At what time of day are you most productive? If it's mornings, schedule meetings and errands during the afternoon block. Learn how you ebb and flow, and schedule your activities accordingly.

3. **Schedule margin** (unplanned time) between blocks. Eat a meal. Go for a walk. Play with your dogs. Put away the laundry. Take your kids out for ice cream. Play a game. Put your feet up. Margin allows you to move into the next block refreshed.

4. **Designate one day each week to take care of business tasks** such as invoicing and following up, planning, bookkeeping, filing taxes, marketing, etc., rather than sprinkling them around your project work throughout the week.

6. Observe a day off every week, also known as a *sabbath*. The idea of sabbath is time dedicated to rest and reflection. Most designers I know, myself included, tend to work long hours during the week and weekends alike. Because of deadlines, unforeseen challenges and unplanned events, we tend to make up for "lost" time on weekends. Creative energy is directly affected by fatigue, illness, and anxiety. Rest and reflective moments are necessary for our overall well-being and allow us to make better decisions. A sabbath rest allows us to shift gears, gain perspective, retain objectivity, and restore balance. It's a day of margin in which we can focus on our Creator and our human relationships and return to the work week refreshed and inspired.

In summary, when pursuing work-life balance don't pursue symmetry. Understand that life consists of seasons and cycles in which priorities, roles, and responsibilities change. Events interrupt our plans and we have to accommodate. Balance via asymmetry in which proportions are unequal and flexibility exists, so that you can manage your life as a whole and prioritize work over personal time, or vice versa as needed, without stressing out.

CHAPTER NINETEEN

HOW TO STAY INSPIRED

Fuel for your thoughts.

There are things we encounter that awake something in us and inspire us: an experience, a revelation, a new insight or piece of information, a connection made, the sight of something beautiful. These things affect us at a heart level so that we desire – in a big way – to do something about it.

Inspiration, by definition, involves mental stimulation that becomes connected to our emotions. It's a combination of thought and feeling which becomes the impetus to take action. The etymology reveals that inspiration originated as the idea of divine guidance, a prompting from the Creator himself.

A secondary definition of inspiration is to draw breath — to inhale — which further alludes to the idea that inspiration does not come from within us, but from beyond ourselves, and we receive it into us and assimilate it. *But it is the spirit in man, the breath of the Almighty, that makes him understand.* — Job 32:8 ESV

We talk about inspiration being sparked or ignited, like a match being struck. In some ways that's an appropriate metaphor. It's a mini-explosion that quickly settles into a steady flame which, unless applied to fuel, will burn out, leaving only a withered, charred stick. But creatives are supposed to be always creating and therefore always inspired, never burning out. As with fire, inspiration needs to be fueled.

In my lifetime of creativity, I've come to know that inspiration does not simply show up out of nowhere. The blank page or screen I face each day is meant to be the start of a great adventure rather than an intimidatingly empty space. I must regularly do those things that keep me inspired and I must stoke the fire through the entire project until it's completed and delivered.

INSPIRATION IS THE ANTITHESIS TO BURNOUT

Burnout is the result of working at something with no ongoing inspiration. The fire that first fueled us to action fizzles out, leaving us to trudge along without vigor or excitement. Inspiration is necessary to start something. Maintenance is required to stay at it and make something of it.

Inspiration can come from anywhere. We can be initially inspired and energized to work on something, but then we need to remain inspired in order to finish the work. This requires intentional effort and focus on an ongoing basis. We're each responsible to maintain our creative energy especially when working with clients. So we must keep our eyes open to notice and observe, reflect on what we've read in order to retain and recall, and be self-aware to notice what catches our eye and what we remember hearing and doing. Inspiration is all around us but we won't recognize it unless we're looking for it.

Inspiration invigorates and energizes us. There's strength in being excited about something. We become eager to get going, take action, get it done. If we're delayed in that effort, or don't begin at all, the inspiration eventually fades and we don't care anymore.

HOW TO STAY INSPIRED

Using the fire analogy, there are a number of actions we can take to stay inspired over the long haul:

1. **Put more fuel on the fire.** Revisit the circumstances that first inspired you. Write the vision down or capture it visually when you are initially inspired so that you can return to it and remind yourself why you're doing what you're doing. I have places that inspire me, and I return to them as often as I can. I look back through old sketchbooks and journals. I hit up museums and exhibits. I go online to study the work of illustrators, master artists, and designers who have influenced my work. I read. I go to movies. I draw. I watch people when I'm out and about. I capture photos of things I notice and add them to my scrap file.* I use my social media platforms quite a bit, searching out words and images that stand out to me.

2. **Put appropriate fuel on the fire.** What inspires me might not inspire you. Know stimulates your thinking and touches your emotions. Remember the second definition of breathing in? We can also breathe in things that can harm us, so stay where your oxygen is. Don't take in anything that's not going to keep you energized.

3. **Keep the fire together.** Whether in person or online, get together with others and share ideas, stories, pain points. Take a class. Engage in some therapeutic scrolling online to see what others are doing. Take a drive or walk to an area you're unfamiliar with, or return to a place that's inspired you in the past.

---

* A scrap file, also called a morgue or morgue file, is a curated collection of visual reference sources organized into folders by topic or category. My scrap file included animal subjects, portraits, color schemes, lettering and typography, vintage signs, autos, landscapes, trees, flowers... anything I might be asked to ow want to draw or paint. Formerly it was housed in several file cabinets. But now it's in digital folders and backed up onto an external drive.

4. **Share the fire.** A single spark can start a massive wildfire. We can remain inspired by inspiring others. When you notice someone else is getting excited about something, encourage and bolster them. Parents to kids, teachers to students, friends to friends and colleagues to colleagues, we keep each other going by sharing and inviting people to share with us.

Inspiration is different for every individual. The key is to know what inspires you — what gets your thinking going, and gives you joy and delight. I appreciate this verse about the joy and strength we experience when inspired: *Then I was beside Him as a master craftsman; And I was daily His delight, Rejoicing always before Him...* — Proverbs 8:30 NJKV

PART 3

MECHANICS

THE WAY IN WHICH SOMETHING IS DONE OR OPERATED; THE PRACTICALITIES AND DETAILS OF AN OPERATION OR SYSTEM.

CHAPTER TWENTY

PLANNING YOUR BUSINESS

Success requires planning.

Creating a plan for your freelance business is one of the first tasks to complete. Your business plan is a roadmap for achieving financial stability and setting appropriate targets. It enables you to hit your goals because it describes your client base and marketing activities, financial goals, identifying risks and considers strategies to overcome them, and is the outline for creating a structured and profitable business. A solid plan bolsters your confidence to make decisions that will help you prosper.

As a creative, it's easy to focus on your craft and neglect the business side of making a living from the work you love. You are, after all, a creative. But when you understand and assimilate the idea that you're actually the owner of a creative business as opposed to being a creative, you need to decide how you're going to thrive. The process of writing a business plan will help to shift your mindset from that of creative to that of business owner.

A written business plan is the starting line to build a freelance business that will prosper, so it should be done early in your set up process. While it won't guarantee you'll succeed, it will help you define what success looks like and channel your decisions in the right direction. Once in place, you'll be able to refer to it, revise it when needed, and follow it as your road map to long-term success.

BENEFITS OF CREATING A BUSINESS PLAN

Before we get into how to write a business plan, let's look at the benefits of having one:

Clarity and direction. A business plan compels you to define your goals, your target audience / ideal client profile, and your service offerings. It's a guide for making decisions to keep your freelance business on track.

Financial management. By deciding on projected income, expenses, and cash flow, you can anticipate your financial needs and avoid unexpected problems. Identifying business goals and objectives enables you to price your services realistically.

Professionalism and Credibility. Using a business plan positions you as a serious professional whether you're pitching to a client, applying for a grant, or seeking collaborative projects. You're less likely to be misclassified as a hobby artist or an employee.

Branding and marketing. Because your business plan helps you define your niche, ideal clients, and key messages, your marketing efforts are targeted and more effective.

Growth and adaptability. A written plan helps you track progress, accomplishments, and pivot when needed. Whether you're adding new services or scaling your operations, your business plan provides a flexible structure for wise decisions and consistent growth.

HOW TO WRITE A BUSINESS PLAN

Although it may seem daunting, writing a business plan is actually fairly simple. You just need to know what the ingredients are. Follow this list of core contents to craft your plan:

Executive Summary
This summary is a brief overview of who you are, the services you offer, and what you aim to achieve.

Services and Offerings
A menu of your creative services (e.g., graphic design, illustration, photography) with descriptions and pricing structure. Go deeper than "I design websites." Carefully consider the business problems you solve for your clients. Your service offerings should address specific needs in the marketplace. This will point back to your vision and mission.

Target Market
The whole world is not your audience. Narrow your target. What industries, demographically and psychographically, do you want to work with? Describe in detail the types of clients you serve or intend to serve.

Marketing Strategy
Include an overview of how you'll reach and attract your ideal clients — website, email, social media, business networking, content marketing, portfolio platforms, etc.? Be the platforms you use are the same your target audience is using.

Competitive Analysis
Understand your competition and the choices your prospective clients have. Who else is offering similar services, and what sets you apart? What's your competitive advantage?

Financial Plan
Include projected annual income, expenses, pricing structures and financial goals. What tools, whether analog or digital, will you use for budgeting and tracking your income?

Business Operations
Describe your workflow, tools, client onboarding process, and how you'll handle administrative tasks (invoicing, contracts, taxes, etc.).

Goals and Milestones
Outline short-term and long-term goals. These can be income targets, client numbers, service expansions, or professional development. Set short-term goals for 12 months and long term goals for three to five years out.

The Small Business Administration (SBA) and SCORE (Service Corps of Retired Executives both offer free online business plan templates you can use as models for writing yours.

Having a business plan will increase your chances of success. You will be better able to anticipate possible problems and mitigate their impact. *The prudent sees danger and hides himself, but the simple go on and suffer for it.* — PROVERBS 27:12 ESV. You'll be able to assess and adjust, track your progress, and know when you've hit your milestones. To stay on track it's helpful to review your business plan once each quarter at minimum and make adjustments.

CHAPTER TWENTY-ONE

BUDGETING FOR FREELANCERS

How to plan your spending when your income isn't steady.

Did you know that the primary reason small businesses go out of business is because of cash flow problems? The same is true for micro businesses and freelancers. *Planning your spending*, both personal and professional, is crucial to maintain a thriving business.

Many freelance creatives are financially illiterate or start out that way. They do okay for a time but end up shutting down because they don't manage their cash and can't pay their bills.

These creatives need to make a substantial shift in how they think about money. The first step to take in making this shift is to actually think about money. We don't go into business to lose money. Businesses should make money. Hobbies, on the other hand, cost money. It's not good to pursue freelancing with a hobby mindset.

THE PURPOSE OF A BUDGET

Creating and maintaining a budget is the basis of managing money. A budget is a spending plan. Without a budget you won't know where your money is going. While many view a budget as restrictive it actually gives you permission to spend your money.

Generally freelancers don't budget because they don't have consistent income — salaries — every month. Income fluctuates. Feast or famine cycles are commonly experienced. How do you budget if you don't know how much you have to spend? Freelancers have to budget differently than employed people. Here's what I figured out:

Budget for each month based on income from the previous month. Because freelance income isn't consistent month-to-month, we can only work with what we actually have on hand. So, plan the budget for July based on what you earned in June. In July, plan the budget for August. This might seem like extra work to create a new budget every month, but if you use spreadsheet software or a budgeting platform, it's actually convenient and easy. Set things up once, and then all you need to do is change out the amounts each month.

Create two versions of your budget: ideal and bare bones. For slow months where income is low, use the bare bones version. This version will only include what's absolutely necessary: mortgage or rent, utilities, food, transportation, healthcare, insurance, necessary software subscriptions, etc. It won't include categories for eating out, buying coffees, buying clothing, entertainment, vacations, events, etc.

Your ideal budget will include everything you spend money on and should include amounts designated for savings, investments, retirement, emergency funds, vacations, sinking funds, and debt reduction. The way you implement the budgets is this: If June was a high-revenue month then design your ideal budget for July. If revenue in June was minimal, create a bare bones budget for July.

Follow the zero dollar budget method. This means that every dollar you bring in is assigned a job to do. You know what's come in and you know where it's going, with no stragglers. If you earn $6,000 in June, that's your budget for July, and expenses and set asides should total $6,000 to zero things out. Total monthly income minus total monthly expenses should equal zero.

BUSINESS BUDGET CATEGORIES

Because your life is a *gestalt* and consists of personal and professional parts, it's a good approach to budget for your whole life. Maintain separate budgets but connect them because you take from the profits of your business to cover your personal and household needs. Your business budget must be separate from your personal budget not only to easily manage your income and expenses, but because the IRS requires it as an evidence of profit motive. Below are two examples of business budgets with expense categories. One is based on regular business operations after launch, and the second reflects start-up costs if you're just launching your business. Neither of these pertain to your household budget.

SAMPLE OPERATING BUDGET FOR YOUR BUSINESS

Rent/Lease	$ ________
Office/Art Supplies (tangibles, consumables)	$ ________
Advertising/marketing/promotion	$ ________
Software subscriptions	$ ________
Internet/phone	$ ________
Utilities	$ ________
Equipment purchase, lease, maintenance	$ ________
Business Insurance	$ ________
Postage/Shipping	$ ________
Transportation/Gasoline	$ ________
Licenses	$ ________
Advertising/Marketing	$ ________
Memberships	$ ________
Professional Services	$ ________
Taxes Set Aside	$ ________
Total Monthly Operating Costs	$ ________
Add profit amount	$ ________
Total Monthly Budget	$ ________

SAMPLE START-UP BUDGET FOR YOUR BUSINESS

When you first start your business there are costs in addition to operating costs involved. Many of these, but not all, are one-time or occasional costs. If occasional, they will end up as part of your operating budget.

Domain Registration	$________
Website hosting	$________
Business License(s)	$________
DBA Filing	$________
LLC/S-Corp Fees/Registration	$________
Rent/lease/office space	$________
Software subscription/purchase	$________
Equipment purchases	$________
Insurance	$________
Legal/accounting services	$________
Business Mentor/Training	$________
Total Start Up Budget	$________

SEPARATE YOUR FUNDS

Open separate bank accounts for your business. Choose a bank or credit union that's familiar with small businesses. Pay business expenses and capture business income with your business checking account. Transfer funds from your business account into your personal bank account to pay household and personal expenses. Don't deposit business income directly into your personal account. If you don't keep your business income and expenses separately from your personal transactions, you can't know if you're actually making any profit. And income tax preparation will be more complicated and time-consuming if you have to locate and separate business and personal expenses in the same account. So, for ease and legal reasons, keep your accounts separate but linked.

IMPLEMENT SET ASIDES

Freelance business owners can be surprised when April rolls around and they discover at the last minute that they owe taxes, so be sure to prepare in advance. From each paid invoice set aside 25% of the amount in a high yield savings account to pay tax obligations. I also recommend working with a tax professional to ensure you have all your deduction bases covered.

The practice of setting aside funds for large purchases as a way to avoid debt is known as **sinking funds**. It's sort of a personal lay-away plan. Set aside small amounts for a specified period of time to cover large expected purchases and expenditures. Sinking funds are used for **planned** future expenses such as equipment purchases, real property down payments, vehicles, education, conferences, etc.

Another set aside is the **emergency fund** to cover **unplanned** expenses. An initial amount of $1,000 should be set aside in a high yield savings account or money market account, and built up incrementally to eventually cover three months of business and life expenses.

Having been in debt for a number of years, I'm a strong advocate for avoiding debt, especially credit cards. If you choose to use credit cards or take out a loan for your business, your money will be obligated first to pay those debts and you'll have less cash on hand to use for your business. You will be less profitable. Be prudent and discerning when making these decisions. Acquiring debt happens in a moment but it can take years to pay it off.

CHAPTER TWENTY-TWO

PRICING YOUR CREATIVE SERVICES

Every project is unique.

Pricing your creative services is one of the most concerning topics among freelancers. Pricing too high scares prospective clients, and pricing too low can put your business in jeopardy.

There is no one right way to price your creative services, nor are there industry standards. There are many factors involved in pricing, and many pricing strategies. The secret to effective pricing strategies for creative freelancers is to follow one method. While flexibility in setting your fees is often viewed as a good thing, utilizing a variety of pricing structures is confusing for you and your clients. It's best to choose a method you're most comfortable with and stay with it. So let's get into the pricing discussion.

PRICING RIGHT

From the client's point of view, pricing is about costs and expenses. They need a piece of visual or written communication and are paying for its creation. From the freelancer's point of view pricing is about lifestyle. How many hours in a day or month do you want to work? How do you charge enough to sustain you business and household yet not be working all the time? How do you use pricing to filter out less desirable clients? How do you get paid what you're worth?

To know how to price your creative services it's helpful to understand what pricing is. Ultimately, it's about value. Business transactions should be a value-for-value exchange. You provide a valuable service resulting in valuable assets, and the client provides value to you in the form of payment. No client wants to overpay. What you need to understand is that **value of the work is determined by the client**, but you can influence their understanding of the value.

Pricing needs to be based on the components and variables of a project, the end usage, the client's ability to make the investment, and your costs of doing business. Every client and project is unique. You may develop the very same types of brand identity assets for two different clients but negotiate two very different budgets — one low and one high — because the needs and abilities of each client are unique. Common factors to consider when setting your creative fees include:

- Scope of work
- Need date
- Size and reach of the client (determines their budget)
- How the work will be used
- How long the work will be used
- Where the work will be used
- Usage rights being transferred
- Business overhead costs
- Your level of expertise
- Your degree of risk in taking on the project

TRADE PRACTICES

General trade practices are the basis for pricing standards. Trade practices are not rates, but the basis for rates; they're the common ways business is conducted in particular industries or regions. For example, a common trade practice for photographers shooting lifestyle is to apply a *mark up* on model fees. These are common trade practices in the visual communications fields:

The **intended use of the work** influences the creative fee. If the design is a piece of key art to be used in a shadow drop for a gaming software company and will enjoy extensive use in a global market, fees will be higher than if the art is used as a digital poster for a local gaming competition.

Freelance creatives charge higher fees — typically an additional 25% to 100% — for **rush work** that needs to be completed in a reduced amount of time.

Expenses reimbursed by the client are marked-up. A mark up is the additional percentage charged on expenses to help ensure a profit. It's the difference between your actual cost and the amount you charge your client. Generally my mark-up ranges from 20% for higher costs to 40% for lower costs.

If a client cancels a project after work has started, and it's not due to any fault of the freelancer, a **kill fee** covering the amount of work completed, plus any expenses, is applied.

Net 30 payment terms — payment is due on an invoice within 30 days of the invoice date — is an industry standard. Some freelancers offer a 10% to 15% discount if an invoice is paid within 10 days. However, I advocate and teach the use of down payments and progressive billing to avoid having to wait to be paid for a project you've already delivered to the client.

Avoid speculative work. These are projects offered by clients in exchange for promised exposure, media placement, or future work — anything that's not monetary compensation. By working on spec you assume all the risk with no guarantee of payment or promises fulfilled. A related scenario is working for a good cause, also known as *pro bono*. A prospective client may request that you work for free because they're a non-profit or other NGO and your reward for doing so will be an increased sense of altruism: "Think of all the people you'll be helping." Pro bono is worthy if it's your choice, but should not be expected by clients.

Creatives are entitled to use the work they create for clients in their **portfolios and marketing** efforts.

FIVE POPULAR PRICING STRATEGIES

Time-based. Whether by the day or by the hour, time-based pricing is where most freelancers start out. This makes sense since most employees are compensated based on number of hours worked. Everyone's used to hourly rates. The key here is to charge appropriately. You may start out in the $20.00 per hour range and, as you gain experience, increase your rate. If you position as a consultant rather than an entry-level, mid-level or senior-level creative, you generally will be able to command a higher hourly rate, ultimately being able to work less hours in a week.

When pricing by the hour, the only way to increase your revenue is by increasing your rate or the number of hours you work. There are only so many hours you can work each day, so this method has its limitations.

Some types of freelancers charge a day rate which is a flat fee for a determined number of hours worked in a day. In charging a day rate you need to define the number of hours the day consists of, and be watchful about overtime.

One problem with time-based pricing is that, as you gain skill and expertise, you tend to complete projects quickly compared to when you started out. So you can leave money on the table (you're penalized) by being better at what you do.

Calculate your hourly rate. You can't based your rate on what an employed creative would earn. You have to ensure that your hourly rate is sufficient to cover both business and household expenses if you're freelancing full time. If you tend to work less billable hours in a week, your hourly rate must increase. You also should consider if you're the only earner in your household, or your spouse/partner is also earning. To figure out your hourly rate, add up your total annual costs plus your desired profit and then divide by total estimated billable hours. Not all working hours are billable hours. You can follow these steps:

Add up all your business expenses for a full year.

Add on a percentage for profit.

Add up your household expenses for a full year (for full-time freelancers).

Estimate the number of billable hours* you will work in a week. If you work an 8-hour day, part of that will be non-billable. Multiply that number of billable hours by 48 weeks (assume two weeks off every year for vacation and holidays) to get your annual total billable hours.

Divide your total cost of doing business (including profit) by the number of annual billable hours to get your hourly rate. For example:

+ Business expenses	$42,000.00
+ 30% profit	$12,600.00
= TOTAL BUSINESS EXPENSES	$54,600.00
+ Household expenses	$64,000.00
= TOTAL EXPENSES	$118,600.00
÷ Annual billable* hours	1,440
= Hourly rate (rounded down)	$ 82.00

* Billable hours are the time you spend directly working on client projects and related tasks. It's the amount of time you charge to a client, and should be tracked.

I'm of the opinion that life is a whole (*gestalt*) consisting of related parts, as described in Chapter 18: The Art Of Balance. Your professional life can't be separated from your personal life. When making business decisions consider the impact on your home and family. This is why, especially if you freelance full time, you have to consider your household needs when setting your creative rates.

Another important consideration about hourly pricing is that you have to track your time to be able to give an accounting to the client when requested. There are apps that help with this.

Project-based pricing. Another popular pricing method is to charge by the type of project. For instance, the design of a 6-page non-commercial web site is set at a certain price. The design of a logo is set at a certain price.

This means you're charging for the *type of work*, not the *time you spend* on it. Clients appreciate this, especially when you offer a menu of projects they can choose from. They also like it because you're not charging more for add-ons or changes, which are inevitable. Unless you get very detailed in what's included in a price, you can end up with less revenue and a lot more work than you expected due to *scope creep* and client-requested *revisions*. Example of a detailed project-based pricing description: *Logo design: includes 3 initial concepts, 1 refinement and 1 final design.*

I've encountered freelancers who publish a menu of creative services and fees on their website. Doing this makes it easy for a prospective client to decide whether to work with you or not, but it also ties you to the published prices, and makes your work a commodity. I recommend that you avoid publishing your rates.

An off-shoot of project-based is **package-based or bundling.** This approach is useful when working on a number of related projects. An example of package-based pricing would be combining logo development, website development, and an email newsletter template design into one project scope to create a package deal. Package deals can be used to attract new projects and clients. They provide the client with an array of related visual communications pieces for one combined price.

Value-based. As an ideal strategy, this method requires that you discuss the full scope of the client's needs up front so that you can offer an informed estimate. Value pricing considers the scope of the work, its use (where, and for how long), the rights transferred to the client, the need date — standard or rush, the complexity of the project, and can even compensate for the degree of difficulty of working with the client. You also will want to learn about the client, their goals, their audience, there position in the marketplace. **Value pricing addresses the worth of your work to the client, not the cost of the work to you or the number of hours you spend on it.** If the client is expecting to yield several million dollars on their product launch utilizing your designs or photos, you price based on a percentage of that figure.

Retainer. In situations where a client has an ongoing need for your creative services, a monthly retainer may be the best option. The client pays a set fee in advance each month, and you work toward using up that fee on whatever projects and tasks are needed. For example, if you regularly design and distribute a newsletter for your client, a retainer becomes regular income for you. Retainer agreements should be specific about the work involved and the expected number of hours or deliverables. Anything not included in the retainer scope is billed in addition to the regular amount. Retainers are usually paid in advance each month, and last three months or longer. The benefit to the freelancer is that you can count on the fee each month — it's steady income — and it's paid in advance, and you get to know the client business well due to the extended time of working together. The benefit to the client is that there is a lot of flexibility as to the type of projects covered, the fee is standardized which is good for their budget, and you give the client priority status.

Retainer agreements are a very viable pricing model. Because the work is ongoing and is paid for up front, your revenue is stabilized. You can work on a la carte projects using value-based pricing with some clients, and on retainer with others, depending on what works best for the client and for you.

Each method described above has advantages and disadvantages. You should carefully consider what works best for you. Being consistent in how you price, rather than changing your approach with each client, reduces stress and saves time figuring things out.

A word to the wise. When a prospective client attempts to bargain for a low price, claiming that you're charging too much, attempt to discover their basis. Take the Socratic approach and ask a few questions such as, "What is that opinion based on?" "Too much compared to what?" "Why do you believe the work is worth less?" If you discern that they really don't value the work, it's best that you refer them elsewhere (perhaps to a crowd-sourcing platform.) Don't waste time trying to negotiate a price with an unwilling client.

Determining your freelance rates is a continual process of evaluating your needs, understanding the markets, and consistently communicating the value you offer. Carefully considering these factors, you can establish competitive, sustainable rates that enable you to thrive as a freelancer.

ESTIMATING

While pricing is understood to be the process of deciding what to require in payment for your creative services, estimating is the process of approximating the total cost of a project, with flexibility built in. An estimate is a ballpark figure, and doesn't necessarily coincide with actual costs and your final invoice amounts. You should always provide the client with an estimate for the project, whether on its own or a part of a larger project proposal or contract. Don't do any work until the estimate (or proposal) is accepted and you have a signed contract in place, preferable with a down payment.

When estimating your creative fees you should always consider your needs and costs including the overhead expenses of running your business. When a client asks you "What do you charge for such-and-such," the best response is to tell them, "I'll email you an estimate." This allows you time to consider the scope of work, the schedule, known expenses, how much profit you want to make from the project, to be able to provide an accurate estimate.

Provide the estimate in writing. Develop a template you can customize for each project and client. Don't rely solely on verbal communications when dealing with money and contract terms.

My practice is to ferret out the client's allocated budget by asking, "My rates for this type of project typically range between this amount and this amount. Does that fit your budget range?" If the client isn't agreeable, kindly decline the project, or reduce the scope of work to fit the budget, keeping the door open for them to get the needed funding and circle back. If the client is agreeable, promise a written estimate or proposal by a specified date.

As mentioned above, estimating considers your creative rates and profit margin, overhead, projects expenses, and schedule, at minimum. In addition to your rates, consider the following types of costs:

Supplies and Materials. Will you need to rent or purchase specific tools, equipment, or consumables to complete the project?

Sub-contractors. Will you need to get extra help to complete the project? For example, models, producers, fabricators, production staff, costumers, set dressers, food stylists?

Professional services. Will you need to use a maker studio, book a retoucher or retouching service, pay an attorney to craft an NDA or model release?

Location costs. Will you need to rent space?

Permits. Are permits of any sort going to be required, such as drone permits, location or access permits?

Shipping and delivery. Will you need a courier service, logistics service, or overnight express shipper to deliver the finished work to the client? Will you need a bulk mailing service?

Travel. Will you need to pay for airfare or rail ticket, rent a car, book accommodations, pay for parking, chargers, or fuel in order to fulfill the creative brief for the project?

In summary, when estimating include your creative thinking/problem-solving, usage rights transferred, number/complexity of deliverables, business overhead costs, and all expenses (with a mark up) necessitated by the project goals.

MARKING UP

When expenses are part of a creative project, especially when the freelancer must outlay for those expenses and be reimbursed by the client, it's customary to charge a **mark-up**. The mark-up percentage is up to you. It typically falls between 10%–35% of the expense amount. For example, if your cost for a food stylist is $350.00, you would bill the client $385.00, reflecting a 10% mark-up. Or if your markup percentage is 25%, you'd bill the client $437.50.

Be cautious about sales taxes on expenses. If you operate in a state that imposes sales taxes on tangible goods, you would add the markup percentage to the total of direct costs plus sales taxes. But then you may owe additional sales taxes on the mark-up percentage. Do your research to understand how your state applies sales taxes. Some types of labor may be taxable, and some types of professional services might be exempt. If you're not located in the United States you may need to consider other types of taxes on your creative services as well as expense reimbursements.

If you choose not to mark-up but bill clients for expenses at cost only, it's known as a *pass through*. Some freelancers bill clients an administrative fee instead of marking up expenses.

The reason for the mark-up goes beyond generating additional revenue. It helps mitigate the *risk* involved when you pay for expenses and are reimbursed by the client. If the client doesn't reimburse you, you're still obligated to pay your suppliers.

I've met a few freelancers who choose to have the client pay their suppliers directly, avoiding the need to pay expenses, mark up, and remit sales tax revenues to the government. There's still the risk they take when the client doesn't pay the suppliers. You're on the hook for the goods or services ordered. There's also the loss of control of the outcome if the client takes over.

There's also a scenario I've experienced a few times in the past in the case of printing, where the client insisted that I use their favorite printer who they paid directly. This isn't directly related to a mark-up on expenses, but it's something you can consider if you find yourself in a similar situation. Often there were extra steps and a learning curve in prepping the files for an unknown printer that weren't necessary when using my qualified printers, and I was unable to recapture the cost of the extra time and prep work. In these cases, because I was not in control of the quality of work or how the mechanical files were handled, I charged the client an administrative fee. I also sent the client a written disclaimer that I wasn't responsible for the quality of printing, color accuracy, press checks or proofing. *Note that I also send this disclaimer any time a client wants to use an online printing service that prints in gang runs where color management isn't possible.*

One final thing about pricing— there's a concept known as the **going rate**. Where you live and work will be a factor in your pricing. If you're located on either coast or in a large metropolitan area, you will likely need to charge more due to the higher costs of doing business in those locations. If you're located in a less populated area, you'll charge less for the same type of project. The going rate is also market-based, meaning that there's a preferred price based on type of industry.

As you can understand, there are many things to consider when deciding what to charge for a project. You don't want to find yourself in the middle of a project and realize you're not charging enough.

CHAPTER TWENTY-THREE

HOW TO PAY YOURSELF

Should you take a draw or salary?

Different business structures have different rules for how owners are compensated. How you pay yourself is based on your business type: sole proprietor, limited liability company or limited liability partnership, or S Corporation. Your business type determines how you are taxed.

There are two methods of paying yourself as a freelancer: by draw, or by salary. If your business is an S Corp, you have to pay yourself a salary or take a profit distribution. If you operate as a sole proprietor or single member LLC, a draw is the method to use. You're unable to be both an owner and an employee, so you pay yourself either by draw or by salary, not both.

PAYING YOURSELF AS A SOLE PROPRIETOR

For the sole proprietor there's no distinction made between the owner and the business. Because you're self-employed, you are prohibited from taking a salary. You can't be an employee of yourself. When you draw from your business profits to pay yourself, there is no tax implication. You don't deduct draws as expenses on your Schedule C because they're considered personal income by the IRS. They're also not taxed. The amounts you draw have no bearing on how much tax you pay on your business profits. You can leave your profits in your business bank account or transfer them to your personal account, and it makes no difference.

A scenario: Amalya, a freelance UX/UI designer, made $60,000.00 in profit from her business. She transferred $33,000.00 to her personal savings account and $7,000.00 into her Roth IRA, leaving $20,000.00 in her business savings account. She won't include the total $40,000.00 draw on her tax return, but she will pay income tax and self-employment tax on the total profit of $60,000.00.

Taking an owner's draw is more flexible than paying yourself a salary because it doesn't require consistent cash flow into your business. You can take a draw when you need to, in whatever amount you need to, and skip it when you don't. You can draw more when business is good and less when there's a downturn.

A point to understand about the owner's draw is that you can't send your business into the negative by taking a draw. For example, if your business made a profit of $8,000 in a month, you can't draw more than $8,000 for that month. You can't put your business into a loss by drawing from it for personal use.

Unlike a salaried job that provides annual cost of living adjustments (COLA), your owner's draw will not be consistent month to month or week to week. Don't try to force the draw into an employee salary model. Draw what you need from your business to cover your household and personal needs, and leave enough in your business to cover its obligations and continue generating profits. Live frugally while you build your business.

PAYING YOURSELF IF YOUR BUSINESS IS A CORPORATION

If you've structured your business as an S Corp, you are an employee of your business. You're the chief officer of the S Corp, but not an owner. Therefore you can't take an owner's draw. The IRS requires you to take a salary, and the salary has to be "reasonable." You can also take a profit distribution in addition to your salary which is taxed as personal income. Your business should be generating enough recurring revenue to be able to pay your salary on a regular schedule — weekly, bi-weekly, or monthly, for example. A fixed salary provides regular income you can count on and is paid on a regular, recurring schedule, in a consistent amount. The salary is a business expense. Your business pays the payroll taxes for you via payroll deductions, and should generate a W2 for you for income tax filing purposes.

PAYING YOURSELF IF YOUR BUSINESS IS AN LLC

As an LLC, you can choose how you want to pay yourself: by owner's draw or by salary. The flexibility and simplicity of drawing from your business makes it a more attractive and practical choice for independent contractors.

HOW MUCH SHOULD YOU PAY YOURSELF

How much to pay yourself can create as much consternation as how to price your services. No one formula applies equitably to every situation. These are some factors to consider:

- What do you need to run your household and care for yourself and your family?
- What do you need to be able to pay off student loans and other debt?
- How much revenue is your business generating?
- What are your business costs?

- Is your business growing or stagnating? Are you charging enough for your services?
- Is your business a part-time (side gig) or full-time (sole source of income) enterprise?
- What's comparable for your industry?
- Do you have other sources of income or revenue?
- What is your income tax obligation?

If you're paying yourself a salary, it needs to be *reasonable compensation* which is defined by the IRS as *the value that would ordinarily be paid for like services by like enterprises under like circumstances. Reasonableness is determined based on all the facts and circumstances.* It's appropriate that freelancers wait to incorporate until they are generating enough consistent revenue to do so.

No one should go into business without the intention to make a profit, whether the business is a part-time or full-time enterprise. If you take too large of a draw, or you take too much in salary, your business may not have sufficient capital to continue operating.

Set a Minimum Threshold. The best way to manage your compensation is to provide for your ongoing business needs and set a minimum threshold to cover your **basic personal/household needs**:

Rent or mortgage(s)	$ ________________
Car payments	$ ________________
Transportation, fuel	$ ________________
Insurances	$ ________________
Phone, internet, utilities	$ ________________
Food	$ ________________
Clothing	$ ________________
Loan and lease payments	$ ________________
TOTAL BASIC NEEDS	$ ________________

Anything that you can live without is not a basic need, such as

- Vacations
- Entertainment, including gaming, streaming, cable TV
- Non-business related subscriptions
- Recreation you have to pay for
- New cars, phones, tablets, computers
- Eating out in any form
- Subscription meal services
- Specialized or high-end clothing

If you need **additional sources of income**, pursue those in addition to your freelancing. Many people hold full-time or part-time jobs while freelancing. There is nothing to be ashamed of for doing that. You need to make a living.

Set some revenue targets. For example, if you're making $50,000 a year right now and getting by but finances are tight, set a goal to increase that income by 10%–20% at minimum each year. Deliberately pursue the business growth that will get you to your financial targets. Don't neglect advertising, networking, and self-promotion. Consider how you can diversify your income sources to bring in more income.

CHAPTER TWENTY-FOUR

RECORDKEEPING FOR FREELANCERS

Business records reveal the health of your business

KEEPING RECORDS

As the owner of a freelance business it's necessary to track income, expenses, profit, and loss. You'll supply these records to your tax pro, for funding purposes, and refer to them if you prepare your tax returns yourself. Budgets, accounting records, and profit and loss statements provide you with an accurate picture of the health of your business. Don't rely on permanent online access to bank statements or tax filings. Keep your records close at hand, and back them up offline regularly.

The types of records you need to keep for your freelance business include the following:

- Accounting records: Account registers for checking, savings, credit cards, loans, leases, and monthly statements.
- Income tax returns for prior years and estimated tax payment receipts
- Business license and tax payment receipts for sales taxes, LLCs, and corporations
- Profit & Loss statements.
- Bank statements.
- Annual income statements – 1099s, W2s
- General ledger A list of income and expense categories and running totals you'll use in preparing your taxes. See below.
- Insurance policies for professional and/or general liability.
- Utility bills if you work from home.
- Rent and lease agreements.
- Mileage A record of miles traveled for business purposes,
- Auto maintenance costs, fuel purchases if you use your car for business purposes.
- Identification numbers including: EIN, business license(s), sales tax license, NAICS code, DUN number

SOFTWARE AND SERVICES

There are a number of ways you can store your records, including online, on your desktop or device, or on paper. I don't recommend any particular digital or analog method, but you consider your own preferences and do your own research to determine the easiest and most convenient option for your situation.

It's important to note that business and home office versions of tax and accounting software will cost more than personal versions. Tax preparation services also charge more to prepare business and self-employed returns than personal returns.

There's no problem with preparing and filing yourself. Once you understand the forms and schedules, it's a fairly simple and easy process, although perhaps tedious, to complete and submit your return on your own.

BOOKKEEPING AND TAX DEDUCTIONS

These are common categories for Schedule C deductions and your general ledger (your accounting "books"). The idea is that each of your business expenses is assigned to one of these categories. This list is not exhaustive. Consult with a CPA or tax advisor to learn what deductions you might take in addition to or instead of these:

- Advertising & Promotion
- Business Insurance
- Health Insurance and medical costs (a percentage)
- Loan Interest
- Credit card interest
- Banking Fees
- Charitable Contributions, Donations, Sponsorships
- Education Expenses
- Equipment Purchases and Leases
- Equipment Repair
- Home Office (requires a dedicated room for business use)
- Internet and Cell Phone
- Legal and Accounting Fees
- Office and Art Supplies
- Qualified Business Income (QBI)
- Rent for office/studio space
- Utilities for office/studio space
- Retirement Plan Contributions
- Payments to suppliers and sub-contractors
- Tax and Licenses
- Travel
- Vehicle (Business Use Only)

Set aside time on a regular basis to do your bookkeeping and account reconciliation preferably at the end of each month. That way you're not trying to record a year's worth of transactions all at once, while you're also preparing your tax return, as I used to do. I don't recommend it.

CHAPTER TWENTY-FIVE

DEBT AND TAXES

Taxes are inevitable, but debt is not.

The first 14 weeks of the year are known in the U.S. as tax season. Income tax filing deadline is April 15 of each year, with some variation if the fifteenth falls on a weekend. Income tax is the amount you owe to the government based on your annual earnings minus tax deductions and credits. As an employee, payroll taxes are deducted from each paycheck automatically and remitted to the IRS, but you have to pay then yourself when you're self-employed.

Your *income tax rate* is based on your tax bracket, which is determined by the *total taxable income* from employment, self-employment, investments, grants, sales of property, winnings, and certain benefits. Be aware that tax laws change frequently. Many freelancers rely on tax professionals and accountants for current information.

Freelancers operating as sole proprietors or single-member LLCs are self-employed and required to make **estimated tax payments** every quarter on April 15, July 15, October 15, and January 15. Estimated payments are based on your anticipated income for the current year. You pay these installments using the IRS Form 1040-ES.

If you're a **sole proprietor**, you report the profit you make from your business as personal income on a Schedule C — a supporting document included with your Form 1040 tax return. Use this schedule to report total income earned and claim business-related expenses to determine your *net income* from your business. The net income is reported on your Form 1040.

If your business is structured as an **LLC** (limited liability company), you are not considered the same as your business, but you choose how you are taxed — as either a sole proprietor or as a corporation.

If your business is structured as an **S Corp**, it is taxed as a separate entity. You'll submit tax returns for your business and personal returns for yourself. The business is responsible for payroll taxes, and you take a salary if you work in the business. The S Corp, LLC, and sole proprietor structures were introduced in Chapter 23: How To Pay Yourself. Whenever you have questions about forms, what's deductible, and how to prepare your tax return, consult an accountant, tax preparer or tax attorney. I am not a financial pro and don't offer legal or financial advice. I offer this information for educational purposes only.

INCOME TAX FORMS

You file tax returns based on your legal business structure. Be sure you know what forms you need:

Sole Proprietorship	Federal form 1040 and Schedule C
LLC	Federal form 1040 and Schedule C
Partnership	Federal form 1065
C Corporation	Federal form 1120
S Corporation	Federal form 1120-S

TAX REFUNDS

While it's the goal of many each year to receive money back from the government as an income tax refund, understand what that means. Getting a refund means you've overpaid your tax obligation throughout the year. You've given the government more than you owe, and receive it back without interest. You're essentially loaning the government your money with no increase on the investment. An alternative strategy (perhaps it's an art) is to neither owe on April 15 nor receive a refund. Don't overpay or underpay. That way your money is yours to use at your discretion throughout the year. To avoid overpaying or underpaying, adjust your deductions if you work a W2 job (you're an employee), and accurately calculate and pay estimated taxes for your freelance business.

PREPARING THE TAX RETURN

The choice of how to prepare your tax return is up to you. About 80% of small business owners rely on professional preparation services or CPAs. If you self-prepare your return, be sure to know what records to keep (previous chapter), familiarize yourself with the forms, and keep detained accounting books. Tax preparation software and platforms walk you step-by-step through the forms and schedules. If you use a professional tax preparation service or CPA, you may be able to deduct that cost as a business expense.

What follows are some common questions and situations related to taxes and income and expense reporting for freelancers:

Reporting 1099-NEC or 1099-MISC Income. Depending on how you are paid (check, ACH transfer, credit card, cash, or payment processor) you may or may not receive a 1099 from a client. This income is reported on your Schedule C as business income, not on your Form 1040. Note that all freelance income should be included on your Schedule C whether or not you receive a 1099.

Full-time job with part time freelance income. Income from employment is reported on your Form 1040. Your employer provides a W2 wage statement which includes the gross amount earned, payroll taxes and deductions for insurances and retirement contributions. Income from freelance work is reported on your Schedule C.

Business mileage deduction. To deduct business mileage and auto expenses (fuel, maintenance, insurance, repairs) you have to keep records throughout the year. Records can be written or app-based. Mileage information is included on your Schedule C, and the deduction is limited to the percentage of mileage that the vehicle was used for business purposes.

Home office deduction. The deduction for a home office requires that it's your only place of business, and that the space you're claiming, whether an entire room or part of one, is used exclusively for business activities. You can't rent a co-working space or office somewhere else as your primary work place and also deduct your home office. But you can deduct the rent or fees for use of those commercial workspaces. You can't deduct for a home office if you use part of your kitchen, bedroom, or family room for your business.

The amount of the home office deduction is the percentage of the total square footage of the home that's used for business.

Salaries are business expenses.

If your business is set up as an S-corp you will pay yourself a salary, with withholding. Your business is your employer and responsible for deducting and remitting payroll taxes on your behalf. Your business will issue you a W2 wage statement for tax reporting purposes.

Cost-of-Goods and Office Expense Deduction

What's the difference between cost of goods sold and office expenses? Cost of goods sold pertains to products you produce and sell, not services. If you sell original artwork or other items you make, your supply costs are included under cost of goods sold. If you run a print store on your website or on a creative platform, the cost of making the prints, packaging, shipping, and other fulfillment expenses come under this category. It also pertains to the cost of inks, paints, substrates, etc., if you sell original artwork.

Office supplies and art supplies are Office Expenses. These can include printer ink and paper, pencils, pens, software subscriptions, credit card fees, sticky notes, tape, X-Acto® knives — anything spent on doing business and creating artwork that doesn't become part of a product you sell, such as if you create original physical artwork and then digitize it for online use. This is an ask-your-accountant-or tax-pro situation due to its complexity.

SELF-EMPLOYMENT TAX

Self-employment tax is a blanket term for two different tax charges: Medicare and Social Security. As an employee, your employer pays half, and the other 50% is deducted from your paycheck and remitted to the IRS on your behalf. But when you're self-employed you are responsible to pay both halves. Refer to Chapter 23: How To Pay Yourself to learn or review the differences in tax obligations between sole proprietor, LLC and corporation.

QUALIFIED BUSINESS INCOME (QBI) DEDUCTION

In 2018 the Qualified Business Income (QBI) deduction was implemented for LLCs, sole proprietorships, S corporations, and partnerships. Small and micro businesses are able to deduct a percentage of their business income. The QBI deduction was originally set to expire at the end of 2025, but was implemented permanently via the One Big Beautiful Bill Act (OBBBA). The deduction amount is 20% of QBI, with a minimum deduction of $400 for eligible taxpayers with at least $1,000 in QBI. As always, consult with a qualified tax or accounting professional.

STANDARD DEDUCTION

The Standard Deduction is based on your tax filing status (single, married filing jointly, married filing separately, etc.) The amount of the Standard Deduction has increased in recent years which means that itemizing deductions on a Schedule A is no longer necessary for many taxpayers. Be sure to study up on changes to tax laws to be able to take full advantage of available deductions.

THE NOTHING OWED, NOTHING REFUNDED PRINCIPLE

My goal has been to not owe any taxes nor not receive a refund when I file in April every year. I've not always been successful with this tactic, but it's still my objective to neither under pay nor over pay income taxes.

Here's my reasoning: If you're overpaying taxes so that you receive a tax refund, you're loaning the government your money interest free. As a result, you don't have that money on hand to work with when you need it. If you underpay your taxes, you'll end up paying more than your obligation because of added penalties and interest.

The best approach, in my opinion, is to pay quarterly installments (see next section) of the appropriate amounts so that you neither pay additional taxes nor receive a refund when you file on April 15.

QUARTERLY ESTIMATED PAYMENTS

Self-employed people make estimated tax payments four times each year in April, June, September and January. The amounts of these installments are based on one's expected total income for that year. By making quarterly payments, you avoid making a "balloon payment" to the IRS in April, and also avoid late payment penalties and interest.

Quarterly estimated payments are not tax filings. When you prepare and file your tax return, the amounts of your estimated payments are subtracted from your total tax obligation. What you pay when filing, or what is refunded, depends on the amounts of the quarterly installments paid throughout the year.

Estimated tax payments should represent around 90% of your prior year's adjusted gross income (AGI) and are submitted with Form 1040-ES, either online or by mail. A general rule of thumb for self-employed freelancers is to set aside 30-35% of your income to pay taxes. Set aside a percentage from every paid invoice into a high yield savings account (HYSA) and designate it for taxes.

A question that comes up from time to time: HOW should you

pay your taxes? For freelancers operating as a sole proprietor or single-member LLC, estimated taxes are considered a personal, not a business, tax obligation. As such, you pay your income tax obligations out of your personal account. If your business is a corporation, it will pay taxes and you'll pay personal income taxes. This is covered in some detail in Chapter 25.

SALES TAXES AND RESALE LICENSES

Sales taxes apply to the sale of actual products and tangible goods. Depending on your creative service offerings, you may be required to collect and remit sales taxes to your state. For example, if you broker printing for a client, you should have a resale license. You buy printing from the printer and re-sell it to the client, usually with a mark-up. If you have a resale license on file with the printer, they won't invoice you for sales taxes. You're responsible to include sales taxes on your invoice to your client. So you collect the sales taxes and remit them monthly, quarterly, or annually to the appropriate state agency.

Not all states have sales taxes, and in those that do the sales tax laws and rates may differ. Every county may have a different tax rate. The percentage you charge in sales taxes depends on the county in which you operate, but you remit to the state. Sales taxes are a deductible expense on your Schedule C.

DEBT AFFECTS PROFITABILITY

Money is a tool. The less of it you have, the less you're able to conduct business. Remember that lack of cash flow is the primary reason why small businesses and freelancers go out of business. Learn financial principles so that you can make wise decisions and accurate calculations.

One of the biggest business-killers for independent creatives is debt. Debt makes you a slave to your creditors. *The rich rule over the poor, and the borrower is slave to the lender.* — Proverbs 22:7. Interest charges are additional funds you pay into someone else's pocket.

That's not helpful for your business or your household.

Some proven practices that help you manage your money are:

Create and follow a spending plan, otherwise known as a budget. When you plan your spending you're in control of your money. Budgeting does not mean you can't use your money. It means you are in charge of how you use it. Some of these were covered in Chapter 21: Budgeting For Freelancers.

Establish values and policies around how you will handle money and funding. For example, you can have a policy about shopping necessary equipment and considering refurbished items. Refurbished items cost less than new, out-of-the box-options. Or you may implement sinking funds — putting money aside to save up for big ticket items. Include these policies in your business plan.

Avoid using credit cards and taking out loans. If you use a credit card, pay it in full each month before interest is charged.

Avoid leasing equipment. Leasing is similar to renting in that you're paying to use and are responsible for something you don't own. Compare ownership costs to leasing costs. Whether it's cars or computers, ownership is usually the more prudent way to go.

Save for big-ticket items. Do all you can to put money aside for big expenses like upgrading your vintage Mac Pro to a Mac Studio or purchasing a 3D printer. Set up a high yield savings account (HYSA) to build funds for future purchases.

Establish an emergency fund. Set aside an amount every month in a high yield savings account and add to this fund until you have two to three months of expenses covered. Then allow it to sit there and draw interest. Determine what constitutes an emergency, and commit to using the funds only for emergencies.

Invest in your retirement. Establish a Roth IRA and contribute to it consistently every month. Mutual funds and high-yield savings accounts allow draws when you need cash, and investments in stocks and crypto can be appropriate long-term strategies. Make an appointment with an investment professional to discuss your goals.

Be generous. Make giving part of your money management. Generosity works like planting seeds. When you plant one seed, it yields more seeds. This is a Biblical principle that works in general. *"Give, and it will be given to you: good measure, pressed down, shaken together, and running over will be put into your bosom. For with the same measure that you use, it will be measured back to you."* — Luke 6:38 NKJV

Pay attention to changes in government policies, tax regulations, and labor laws. Know what's going on in your state and federally so that you can make wise decisions and avoid penalties for non-compliance.

Paying only what you owe in taxes, staying out of debt, stewarding your money, and being consistent with your business policies can combine into a thriving business and prosperous life.

CHAPTER TWENTY-SIX

FREELANCE CONTRACTS

Contracts protect the freelancer and the client.

Because pretty much everything in our culture and commerce runs on design and other forms of visual communication, the role of the visual communicator is more in demand than ever, and also more misunderstood than ever. Misunderstanding is reflected in how many freelance creatives are treated by clients operating under false assumptions that they are employees or personal assistants, and that the client is purchasing everything when commissioning the services of a independent creative professional.

Freelance contracts clarify the creator-client relationship and establish expectations before the work is started. We need to be very clear about why they are being contracted to do a project. We also should make sure our clients understand our processes and how the working relationship is structured. The responsibility of maintaining a healthy working relationship is the purview of both you and your client.

HEALTHY CLIENT RELATIONSHIPS BEGIN WITH WRITTEN CONTRACTS

Written contracts describe the project, deliverables, specifications, schedules, terms of service, and ownership. There are different varieties of freelance contracts, but I'm going to focus here on three specific project-based contracts. Before I dive in, I want to first establish this as a disclaimer: I am not an attorney. I am not offering legal advice. If you need legal advice you should seek the counsel of an attorney who practices in business and intellectual property law.

When you first meet with your prospective client, the discussion of the project should center on what the client wants to accomplish with the work you create, how the work will be used, creative fees, expenses, and terms of service. Address all expectations and requests. You will use this information to write a proposal and contract for the project. You'll also use this information in a design (creative) brief.

You should write and offer the contract because it needs to be based on your business practices. Boiler-plate contract templates consistently come up short when it comes to creative work and defining your independent status. So write your own contracts. Develop a standard template you can customize for each client.

When your client is an agency, design firm, publisher, or government agency, it's likely they will offer the contract to you. You should then expect to negotiate terms. Read every contract thoroughly. While you don't necessarily need to have an attorney on retainer, it's a very good idea to consult with one in these cases.

TYPES OF CONTRACTS

There are three basic types of freelance contracts that you might work with: the buyout, work-for-hire, and rights managed.

When you're creating intellectual property, copyright is involved. Copyright is defined as *the exclusive legal right of a creator to print, publish, perform, film, or record literary, artistic, or musical material, and to authorize others to do the same.* Copyright and usage rights must be transferred in writing. So you need a written contract of some sort in order to transfer any rights to your client.

Copyright automatically belongs to you as the creator, and you transfer part or all of your copyright to the client. So when you are dealing with a rights managed type of contract you are considering how your work will be used by the client, how widely it will be used, and for how long.

RIGHTS-MANAGED CONTRACTS

Rights-managed contracts include limited-use, multiple-use, and full-use options. You want to give the client what they need, but not more than what they need.

Limited use places strict limits, constraining use in a variety of ways. For example, a limited rights contract can specify a particular region; a particular medium such as print or digital. It can specify a platform (ex., for use on a particular website only); it can allow one-time print reproduction rights in a particular magazine or journal; or it can allow a time limit. You can be very specific as to what rights you are transferring to the client. In all cases, you retain the original rights of authorship. If you've ever purchased the license to use software, stock photography or fonts, you've encountered limited use licensing (whether or not you've actually read the entire license agreement.)

Multiple use contracts allow for broad scope of use. Multiple rights are appropriate for clients who will use the work extensively in branding building and marketing over long periods of time. You may require higher fees for multiple rights contracts because your work will be used extensively.

With rights-managed contracts you need to know what your client needs. If you create a logo, the client needs full use of that intellectual property and the ability to use it at will for as long as needed. If you are creating a brochure, you need to consider if it's print, digital or both, how many will be distributed, where, and for how long.

Rights can be exclusive or nonexclusive. An example of exclusive rights is a logo that's designed for the client's exclusive use, and you would not sell the logo to another entity. *Non-exclusive rights* means that what you create for a client may be sold or used elsewhere (by you, not the client) in a non-competing market.

Selling your original art files (PSD, INDD, AI, for example) or original physical artwork, is not included when selling rights. **Ownership of the original artwork or working files is separate from the right to use and reproduce the work.** You can sell original artwork and retain all rights to it, and vice versa.

Unlimited rights means that the client is purchasing all rights to use the final designs in all places at all times on all media and platforms. The creator of the work (you) retains the original copyright, and may sell use of the work to others in unrelated industries. Unlimited rights is also known as **all rights**.

Exclusive unlimited rights means that the creator cannot sell the use of the work to any other party. Currently, under US copyright law, unlimited rights can revert back to the creator after 35 years upon written notice. With both unlimited rights and exclusive unlimited rights the creator may use the work in their own self-promotion, and the original art files and preliminary work can be sold separately.

THE BUYOUT

Under a **buyout** agreement, the client's expectation is that the original copyright is actually sold. Usually you don't want to do this, because you will lose all control and all ability to gain additional revenue from your work. Additionally, you're not able to showcase it in your portfolio or use it for any sort of promotional purposes without permission from the client, because you essentially have given up all your rights to and authorship of the work.

Buyout is a vague concept, full of assumptions and can often be interpreted in ways detrimental to the creator of the work. Instead of a buyout, offer unlimited (all) rights.

WORK MADE FOR HIRE

Work-made-for-hire (work-for-hire) contracts are standard in some industries such as film and publishing, where you're contributing to a larger collective work or their use is standard, but it's best to avoid them otherwise.

Work-for-hire puts the creator at a disadvantage by automatically establishing the client as the owner of the work and in total control of all usage. It gives authorship and ownership to the commissioning party. The creator has no rights to it. Certain conditions must be met for a work to be a work-for-hire. Employed creatives, being part of an organization, do not have the authority to claim copyright for the work they create in their role as employee. Their work belongs to the employer.

But freelancers are independent contractors. When a freelancer enters into a work-for-hire agreement, they are same as employees but without benefits. The freelancer is unable to realize additional income from the work they create if it's created under a work-for-hire agreement.

AVOIDING WORK-FOR-HIRE RELATIONSHIPS

It's best to avoid work-for-hire if you are an independent contractor. Conflicts can arise when clients assume that you are working for hire and expect full ownership and even authorship status of your work. This is one reason why you need to use written contracts.

I once had this happen with a long-time client who moved to another region and decided to work with a local designer there. She requested that, along with the final files, I hand over my working files so that she could give them to her new designer. I refused, and she countered, stating that she had paid for them. But she hadn't. My contract terms of service included who owns the working files and designated an additional fee be paid to purchase the working files. All I had to do was to enforce my contract terms.

Under current US copyright law there are particular conditions that make something a work-for-hire. There must be a written contract stating that the work is a work-for-hire, the work must be specifically commissioned, and it has to be created for a collective work. If all three conditions are not met, it is not a work-for-hire.

Since work-for-hire agreements put you at a disadvantage in terms of rights and authorship, you should avoid them. If it's an industry standard, you should be compensated well enough so that loss of potential income is offset by the amount of money you earn from the project.

FREELANCERS SHOULD ALWAYS USE WRITTEN CONTRACTS

Ownership — copyright — is a common assumption among clients, and is the most compelling reason why freelancers should always use written contracts. A contract puts everything in writing so that everyone knows the expectations, the terms, what rights transfer, when they transfer, and when they revert. A contract protects the client from wrong assumptions and protects the freelancer from being assumed upon.

I strongly recommend that freelancers who create intellectual property for their clients acquire a basic understanding of copyright law. This knowledge will protect your revenue and reputation.

If you are a freelancer who does not use written agreements as a normal course of business, you should begin doing so with your next project, and that you begin to educate yourself about copyright and contractual relationships.

INCLUDE COPYRIGHT TERMS IN YOUR CONTRACTS

Section 204 of the United States Copyright Law specifies that **copyright does not transfer unless it's in writing, and it has to be the copyright owner who is making the transfer.** There is only one other way to transfer a copyright and that is via a legal judgment.

Here is the law as stated at copyright.gov*:

> *204. Execution of transfers of copyright ownership*
>
> (a) A transfer of copyright ownership, other than by operation of law, is not valid unless an instrument of conveyance, or a note or memorandum of the transfer, is in writing and signed by the owner of the rights conveyed or such owner's duly authorized agent.
>
> (b) A certificate of acknowledgment is not required for the validity of a transfer, but is prima facie evidence of the execution of the transfer if—
>
> > (1) in the case of a transfer executed in the United States, the certificate is issued by a person authorized to administer oaths within the United States; or
> >
> > (2) in the case of a transfer executed in a foreign country, the certificate is issued by a diplomatic or consular officer of the United States, or by a person authorized to administer oaths whose authority is proved by a certificate of such an officer.

In conclusion, never work without a written contract. It is your safety net and lifeline in the case of a misunderstanding or dispute. The contract also helps educate your client — the majority of your clients will have no clue what they are actually paying for when they work with you. It's your responsibility to educate them. By signing a contract the client agrees to the deliverables, schedule, budget, and terms of service, and has the means by which they can hold you accountable to complete the project.

A written contract assures that both parties come away with what they both need — compensation on the one hand and permission to use the work on the other.

Be sure to check out the Terms Of Service section of the Appendices for examples of contract terms and clauses to include in your own contracts.

---

* https://www.copyright.gov/circs/circ30.pdf

CHAPTER TWENTY-SEVEN

PRINCIPLES FOR NEGOTIATING

Freelance creatives must be able to skillfully negotiate contracts and project offers

Coming to terms about a creative project requires agreement between you and your client. The process by which you arrive at a mutual understanding is known as *negotiation.*

Negotiation is the process of obtaining something or bringing something about by discussion; reaching an agreement or compromise by discussion. The word has Latin origin: *Negotiari* refers to something being done *in the course of business.* An obvious clue from the definition is the fact that negotiation requires conversation.

Negotiating is a necessary part of doing business. Both parties pursue a beneficial outcome for themselves. The client pursue the most they can for the least cost, and the freelancer pursues the highest price for the least amount of effort. Negotiation isn't a win-win pursuit. While the ideal is that both you and your client are equally satisfied, it's up to you to protect your livelihood. Compromise is required to come to terms, but be cautious about what you concede to during a bargaining conversation. You should be straightforward and professional but avoid being taken advantage of.

While you don't want to work in exchange for "exposure" or the promise of future projects, you will want to consider certain concessions if you want to win the project. Always pursue a reasonable profit, but consider that value isn't necessarily determined by money alone. The expansion of one's portfolio, the high-visibility nature of a client or project, and the amount of creative freedom, are all viable reasons for adjusting price.

As with most skills, negotiation is learned. You become better at it through practice. As soon as you begin discussing a project, you are negotiating. Both you and your client have goals for the project, and the point is to bring your goals into alignment. In a successful negotiation both client and creative maintain respect for each other.

WHAT IS NEGOTIABLE?

Required creative services. The client may have initially requested a logo but in the course of your discovery conversation(s) you determine they need an entire re-brand in order to achieve their objectives. You need to know why you're creating the work in order to know what to create.

Rights Transferred What rights will transfer to the client, when will they transfer, and for how long? How will the work be used? Consider media, platforms, geographic location and duration of use. A logo and brand identity will require an all rights, while an e-commerce video for use on social platforms to promote an event may have a 90-day duration, and may not be used on the client's YouTube channel.

Deliverables. What deliverables are you creating for the client? Specify each item and include quantities, formats, print runs, etc.

Creative Rates. What will you charge the client for your services?

Schedules/Deadlines When is the work needed?

Value of the Work. What results does the client hope to achieve with the work? What are their business objectives? Focus on the results of the deliverables instead of the deliverables themselves because the client can always obtain a deliverable at less cost.

Depth/Degree of Difficulty How much research will be required to develop concepts and final designs? How many client meetings and creative reviews will be necessary? Will the project require strategy sessions? Is there one person with approval authority or are you expected to work with a committee?

Future work. Will the project promote you in the markets you serve? Will it help you attract higher-value clients in the future?

NEGOTIATION STRATEGIES

Your primary tool for negotiation is your expertise. If the client perceives you as an expert with abilities they don't possess or can't easily source, you have an advantage and your fees are non-negotiable. Few people question an attorney's retainer or a mechanic's hourly rate. It's not that way with freelance creatives. To position as an expert use your work, your successes and your process to attract the attention of potential clients. **Your expertise is your leverage.** If you are discussing a project and negotiating terms, your client has already determined that you're an expert.

Establish (ahead of time) your absolute, bottom-line minimum rate and requirements, and your ideal rate and requirements for a project. The *Minimum Acceptable Rate* (MAR) is the lower-end boundary that you will not cross. When deciding what that rate will be, consider your overhead expenses, degree of difficulty in working with the client, taxes, project expenses, schedule, complexity, and amount of time the project should take.

Then decide on your ideal rate based on everything the project entails, your level of expertise, and the overall value you provide to the client. Your ideal rate should be significantly higher than your MAR to give you flexibility. The ideal rate and the MAR are *anchors* for your negotiation. Anything in between becomes acceptable.

Allow the client to answer the money question first. Before you disclose your ideal rate, ask the client, "What is your budget for this project? What are you willing to invest?" Their answer should fall within your two anchors, or above your top anchor, and will give you an understanding of how the client values the work.

Do not compete on price. Compete on expertise and experience. A client will always be able to find someone who charges less. Be aware of what your competition charges, what they do, and the level of their work (excellent, average, mediocre.) Competing on excellence and value requires that you establish your reputation outside of the negotiations. Grow your skill, gain experience, and brand your business to target the clients you want to attract. The lower the quality of your work, the more competition you will have.

What is the going rate for similar work done by similar freelancers and firms in your area? In the client's area?

Consider the non-financial benefits. Will this project lead to increased exposure with your target market? Will the client refer you to colleagues and influencers in their industry?

What is the **potential for future work** with the client? Negotiating a "get to know you" rate on a first project may be advantageous if you are assured that there will be more work from the client in the near future. However, keep in mind that assurance is not reality. In my experience, the "more work in the near future" promise has seldom manifested. Reducing your rate to secure a project only sets up expectations you'll be obliged to meet in the future. Be wary.

NEGOTIATION TACTICS

Just as the client is interviewing you, you need to interview the client. By researching the client and their industry up front you'll be able to ask strategic questions. These are aspects of a solid strategy that can lead to agreement:

Research the client. Obtaining background information on the client's business is simply a matter of searching online: LinkedIn, their web site, social media. Investigate what the client is doing currently, what problems you observe with their visual and/or verbal messaging, and think about ways you can solve those problems. Bring your conclusions to the negotiating table.

Research the industry. What are the trends and pain points in the industry the client serves? What are the client's competitors doing well and what are they doing poorly?

Ask the right questions. Just in discussion with the client you will have already done some discovery and have collected some facts. The information you learned in your research is the basis for further inquiry. It also lets the client know that you are aware of their enterprise and are asking intelligent questions. This puts you in a position of strength. A couple of examples:

> "I understand that your industry has been experiencing some supply chain disruptions. How is that affecting your sales and customer service?"

> "In doing a graphic audit of your current web site, I noticed that it's not meeting accessibility standards. You're probably losing visitors, which means you're losing customers. What do you think about that?"

Find out the client's needs. You want to learn about their ideal customer profile, their geographic reach (local, regional, national, international, worldwide), how they will use the work you create, how soon they need it. Look for opportunities to up-sell or cross-sell. Example: For several years I designed, edited and produced a monthly news magazine for a trade association. The client had been investing in printing and mailing to more than 2,500 members, and these costs were increasing substantially. I suggested changing to an online version, and designed, edited and managed the web-based edition. My role with the client and my fees were increased during my tenure with them.

Treat the client as a partner, not a boss, and the project as a joint venture. "We're working on this together." Establish a peer-to-peer relationship.

WHAT TO AVOID WHEN NEGOTIATING

Don't discount your creative fee to fit a low budget. Discounts devalue your work and that of your creative colleagues. Instead, modify the scope of work to fit the client's allocated budget.

On occasion, and especially if you're starting out, you'll work with low-budget clients. No matter what the budget restraints are, the key is to avoid discounting your fee to accommodate. Instead, reduce the scope of work, either by eliminating, postponing, or substituting deliverables:

Reduce the number of concepts you develop.

Reduce the number of creative reviews and revisions.

Reduce the number of deliverables. Discuss and prioritize alternatives. Eliminate or table the least important pieces.

Limit the geographic distribution of the work.

Limit the duration of the rights being transferred. Designate a specified date the usage rights revert back to you.

Be willing to decline a project and move on. The client may come back and agree to your full rate, but if not, you haven't lost anything except some negotiating and research time.

Don't agree to add-ons, also known as scope creep. Here's an example of an add-on request and how you might respond:

Client: "While you're doing the web site, can you add a logo? I don't have a logo. You can create it and then just add it to the top so people will know it's my company."

Designer's response: "Sure. I can create a logo for you for between $X.XXX.XX and $X.XXX.XX. That will be a separate project and one that should be done first before I develop your web site."

Client's response to Designer's response: "Can't you just do it as part of the web site?"

Designer: "Developing an effective logo requires thoughtful strategy. It is foundational to your branding program. I'll submit a separate proposal for the logo project."

Don't agree to an exact amount verbally. It's better to suggest a range or ballpark amount. For example: "My fees for designing a web site generally range from $X.XXX.XX to $X.XXX.XX, depending on what features, complexity, and functionality you need." Put an exact amount in writing only when you have gathered all the information about the project.

Don't do work in exchange for a credit line, exposure, or the promise of paid projects in the future. Keep the value-for-value principle in mind and do what's best for your business. The only exception to this is an in-kind sponsorship for a non-profit. Be sure that the organization understands the full value of your services, that you have a written agreement for the sponsorship including their 501(c)3 number, and that you follow up to enforce the terms of the sponsorship.

Don't rush. Even when you come to an agreement, take a day or two to consider it before you submit your contract. If the client is supplying the contract, read it through carefully several times, and ask an attorney to look it over if you need to. Wait a day or two before signing. Time will give you perspective and increase your objectivity.

Don't ignore red flags. If anything about the client makes you uncomfortable decline the project. Do not agree to anything you're not comfortable with.

Don't chase a prospective client. A prospect may go silent or become unresponsive, which may mean they have changed their mind, found someone else, or cannot proceed with the project. If they do not respond to your first follow up query, do not pursue them. Don't offer to work for less and throw in your firstborn if they'll give you the project. Let them go and turn your attention to attracting your best clients. Clients who don't communicate are not your best clients.

BE PROFESSIONAL

Your best approach to negotiating is to be regarded as a trustworthy, professional peer by the client. Be specific, be confident, be a problem-solver. Clients naturally look out for their own interests, and have been known to reveal a larger budget if they understand the quality and value of the work you'll create for them.

Negotiations are not arguments. Although you and the client will differ on many points, this process is not a debate in which one or the other party needs to prevail. Work for the best possible out come yourself. Once you come to agreement, put the agreement in writing in the form of a detailed contract.

CHAPTER TWENTY-EIGHT

WORKING WITH CLIENTS

Cultivating successful working relationships

When working with clients relationship is primary. You don't have a business unless you have clients. So clients are essential to your business and livelihood.

It's important to set the tone with open communication and straightforward business practices. Your ability to work with your clients requires mutual respect for each others' knowledge, expertise, and roles. Setting the tone is to manage expectations, to follow through, and to follow up, and this actually begins at the initial point of contact — the inquiry. As you learn what your client is seeking to accomplish, decide on the project scope and deliverables, go through the negotiation and contract process and on-board the client, you're developing the working relationship. You're developing trust and loyalty with your client, as well as your professional reputation.

The work products you create for your clients are communications assets necessary to their overall business strategy. Your clients are trusting you to deliver what they need at the highest quality and effectiveness. This means that you always keep your clients' best interests in mind throughout a project. These are some best practices for working and building trust with clients:

Learn and speak their language. They're not designers, artists or creatives. They don't have to learn your language. But as a fellow business owner you should learn the terminology of the business world so that you can understand the needs of your clients.

Explain your creative process. Share the steps you take, the type of research and inquiry you do, what the ideation phase is all about. They're usually interested in how you solve their problems.

Communicate consistently. Let them know where you are in the process. Be flexible with communication channels. If your client prefers text message over email, accommodate that.

Learn your clients' goals. What does the work need to accomplish for them? What's the reason for the project at this time?

Don't assume. Ask questions. Ask their opinion.

Be faithful. Deliver on what you promise, but don't over-promise.

Communicate and enforce your boundaries. For example, if your client messages you at 9:45PM but you've clearly stated that you're not available in the evening hours, don't respond until you're back at work. But respond as soon as you can.

Be accommodating, but don't compromise your policies and practices. If it's easier for your client, use digital team collaboration tools.

Defer to your client as the expert in their business and industry. Expect them to respect you as the expert in your role. Discuss approaches and purposes for the creative assets you're developing for them.

WHEN A CLIENT IS HIGH MAINTENANCE

In any relationship personalities matter. It's possible to be working with a client who turns out to be incompatible with you in a number of ways. These areas can include work ethic, communication style, world view, management style, emotional intelligence, and approach to budget (are your services considered a cost or an investment?) You can't fully know until you're in a working relationship and concerns begin to manifest.

Even if a client turns out to be difficult, do your best work, avoid complaining and taking things personally. If you determine it's best to end the working relationship, do so in a gracious and professional manner. Complete the project. Provide them with what they've paid for. Thank them for the opportunity to work with them and wish them good success.

If it's not feasible to complete the project, be direct in telling the client it's not a good fit, recommend other options for them, and wish them well. Resist the temptation to complain to others about the client. Acknowledge your role in the failure of the relationship, and take time to reflect on how you can change your policies and practices to avoid similar situations in the future. For example, having experienced a few clients who didn't pay my invoices, I implemented a policy of requiring a signed contract and a down payment.

Understand that **no client relationship is perfect**. Determine what your needs and non-negotiables are before submitting a project proposal or contract. If you get into the middle of a project and the relationship goes sideways, **seek to resolve the problems to the best of your ability**. When that's not possible, notify the client that you're resigning the project and release them in writing. Leave well or you may carry the same trouble into your next working relationship.

In everything, be grateful for the clients you have. The good ones are a blessing, and the not-so-good ones hone you, reveal your weaknesses and errors, and teach you. Treat others the way you want to be treated (paraphrase of Jesus' famous admonition recorded in MATTHEW 7:12.)

CHAPTER TWENTY-NINE

DIVERSIFYING REVENUE STREAMS

As I shared in a previous chapter, there are risks one takes when traveling the freelance road. In regard to profitability, we place a great deal of responsibility onto our clients, that they'll respond to our marketing efforts and pay our invoices. There's a certain amount of uncertainty when taking on a new client and starting a new project. We hope all goes well and that we'll receive value in exchange for the value we give.

Something I decided to do and recommend to you for stabilizing income is to do more than serving clients only. Diversifying your income sources alleviates much of the financial pressures we all face, and mitigates your risk. Once you become established in working with clients and your project queue is consistent, consider how you might add more income streams. Having multiple sources of revenue stabilizes your income and provides other outlets for your creative drive. It offers exploration of new markets for your work, enhances existing skills and builds new ones, and can lead to increased earning potential. In short, it helps you beat the feast or famine cycle.

In investigating ways to diversify, keep in mind how you can serve people with your work. How will customers benefit from your efforts? Also keep in mind that, diversifying requires additional branding, marketing plans, graphics and content calendars, and possibly additional websites and portfolios. In managing your time, consider how you will add new responsibilities into your schedule.

WAYS YOU CAN DIVERSIFY YOUR INCOME SOURCES

Offer complementary (not complimentary) creative services that enhance your existing offerings. If you' re an illustrator, add on design services as I did. If you're a photographer, add retouching or drone photography services. Complementary services can require you to develop new skills, and will increase your value.

License your work to manufacturers, marketers, publications, and other brands for use on their products and platforms in exchange for licensing fee or royalties.

Sell fine art prints. Offer giclée prints on your own website or a sales platform. Illustrations, designs, portraits, and photographs are all options for selling limited edition prints to collectors and aficionados. For example, one of my students pursued a nomadic lifestyle and traveled by van to every U.S. national park, and subsequently designed travel posters for each which he sells through print-on-demand platforms.

Participate in community art shows and fairs sponsored by municipalities and organizations. Shows require planning, preparation, and time, but can be quite lucrative.

Create design templates and mock-ups to sell through online marketplaces such as Design Cuts, and Thrive Creative Market.

Engage in affiliate marketing. Review and recommend products, tech, books, and gear you already use. You can earn commissions when people make purchases through your affiliate links on your websites and social media. Affiliate marketing requires a disclosure statement and sometimes has platform and application limitations. For example, you may have permission from Amazon to include affiliate links with a YouTube video but not in your email newsletter.

Sell merchandise. Create your own apparel and product designs to sell through print on demand purveyors such as Society6 and TeeSpring.

Create and sell coloring books. If you're an illustrator or artist, publish your preliminary or final line drawings as adult or children's coloring and educational books. Develop characters and story lines to provide children with story books they can color themselves.

Create and sell paper goods. Journals, planners, calendars, washi tapes, sticker sets, inserts, represent a growing and enthusiastic market.

Launch a subscription service. Utilize platforms such as Patreon, Medium, YouTube, and Substack to offer exclusive content to paying subscribers. Content can include behind the scenes (BTS), tutorials, process clips, early access to new products, surveys, exclusive downloads, or discounts on your merchandise, in order to build a reliable audience and generate recurring income.

By diversifying your income sources you can protect against periods of slow work and enjoy a more consistent cash flow. Diversification minimizes risks of unexpected events, market changes, and project cancellations. You can increase your earning potential by engaging with different markets and customers. You can pivot and capitalize on new opportunities and emerging trends. And with multiple income streams, you can be more selective about the clients you work with and the projects you take on, focusing on those that will propel you forward instead of accepting a less desirable project out because you need the money.

PART 4

MESSAGE

CRAFTING AND GROWING YOUR REPUTATION

CHAPTER THIRTY

THE ART OF INFLUENCE

Authenticity, integrity, and follow through matter.

To be successful, you need to be influential. Influence can be positive or negative, and everyone has influence. The key for success as creative freelancers is to be strategic in growing your influence. Decide what you want to accomplish, and do the things that will influence that outcome.

Influence is the capacity to have an effect on something or someone. You don't need to be, and in fact can't be, influential with everyone, but you do need to influence your target audience. As a creative entrepreneur, you want to make an impact in your sphere or you will not remain in business for long. When you are influential it's a given that you are also attractive to your clients. When you complete a job for a client, and you did it well, others will notice. If you were able to pull it off for Company A, you can certainly pull it off for Company B.

INFLUENCE IS BUILT OVER TIME

By creating work for clients that helps them achieve their goals, you are building your own reputation. As you help others become successful, you create your own success in the process. John Maxwell, author, speaker and coach who focuses on leadership and influence, wrote, "A successful person finds the right place for himself. But a successful leader finds the right place for others."*

Strive to be a leader who assists others in their successes. As a creative entrepreneur, you understand the value of your talent and expertise. You provide necessary services that fulfill the needs of specific clients. One reason why you want to be influential is because you want to positively affect outcomes for others. A non-profit client will not meet its campaign goals without the design of appeals and collateral. A restaurant owner won't attract a new clientele without strategically-designed website and marketing campaigns. A craft brewery won't get its product into the marketplace without the photography that will help tell its story and convey the enjoyment of drinking their beer. When you take this approach to your work, you will influence the results for others.

INFLUENCE IS NECESSARY FOR YOUR BRAND

While your brand as a creative entrepreneur is not limited only to influence, it's a starting point for building your reputation in your marketplace. Influence has become the driving force in buyers' choices because there are myriad options and competitors in all market sectors. You are not the only creative expert in your field. Your prospective clients have choices of who they work with. Given those options why would they choose you? It might appear that you

---

*https://www.linkedin.com/posts/officialjohnmaxwell_leadership-always-has-been-and-always-will-activity-7138649435688919040-W2Xg/

should follow the latest trends and emulate what others are doing. If they're successful you can be, too. But this is no longer playing out. Your competitive advantage in the marketplace is your uniqueness. What you bring to the table that no one else can is your primary avenue for influence. In short, don't be like everyone else. Be yourself. Capitalize on your differences.

BE INTERESTED

In his influential book, *How To Win Friends and Influence People*, Dale Carnegie wrote: "You can make more friends in two months by becoming interested in other people than you can in two years by trying to get other people interested in you."

Because they have the power of choice, your current and prospective clients have the power to choose they will be more likely to work with you if they perceive that you can help them grow their enterprises. I've identified five key areas in which you can be strategic about building influence to attract clients:

1. Be authentic. Know the value of your talent and expertise, and also the limits of your knowledge and skill. Where are you in relation to everyone else who does what you do? What are your strengths and weaknesses? In what ways do you stand out from the everyone else who does what you do? What is your value promise, and how do you deliver it? Also, be a person who can be trusted. Act with integrity, following through on what you promise.

In areas where you can create exclusivity, you can increase your value. For example, if you work with just a few clients, if you only work on retainer, if you only accept this or that type of project, you are building value. Become somewhat scarce.

Don't take on every project that comes your way. Be selective, willing to walk away from a project offer. Doing the right kind of work with the right kind of client increases your influence. Whether you are a specialist or generalist, stay within the flow of what you do best. Don't roam into unfamiliar territory simply for the money.

Stay in your own lane, but be able to recommend others. Get to know people with expertise in the things you don't do and recommend them. I worked with a guy who wrote PHP code for a website project. He was insightful, quick to turn things around, and not at all condescending to me as a designer. I'd work with him again any day, and recommend him. He has influence with me.

2. Bring your value into your relationships. When your clients ask to work with you, or your colleagues ask you for advice, you have influence. A good approach to business relationships is to provide answers that are practical and provable.

Be others-focused. The ancient principle that it is more blessed to give than to receive is still true. It is one of those natural laws that never changes. To the extent that you give to others, you will receive, and with interest. I'm not talking about working for free, because another ancient principle also is true: the worker deserves his wages. Give value and receive value in return.

What can you give away? Good advice. Alternative approaches. Insights. Information. Did you just receive something in your notifications or read something favorable online that pertains to a client? Share it. The simple fact that you were thinking about them beyond the project speaks volumes and helps cement connection.

Consider the impact you are have on people. What is the logical outcome of this action or these words? Will your words build up or tear down? Your influence is affected by how you talk about people to others. When a prospective client complains to me about other designers they've worked with, my red flag radar starts beeping.

3. Follow through. Did you promise a first review on this date? Did you agree to find an answer for that question? Did you suggest meeting at noon for lunch next Tuesday? Do it. As much as it is up to you, keep your word. In a culture where lack of follow through is common, the simple act of doing what you say you will do creates positive surprise. People notice that, and remember you for it.

Although no one follows through on every promise made, if you build your professional and personal reputation around keeping your word, you will become known and trusted for it.

4. Listen carefully and pay attention. When conversing with clients and colleagues, be attentive to what they are saying. Observe body language, facial expressions, and tone of voice. Look for clues that will give you deeper insight into their situation. Asking relevant questions, giving feedback, and even summarizing what they've said shows that you were listening, which is huge. It demonstrates that you care about their concerns.

5. Become a peer, and then elevate the other person. Anytime a creative — or any person for that matter — is on the short end of a working relationship, they cannot impact the outcome. It's all in the hands of the other person.

When you come into a working relationship as a peer — on the same level and equal footing — you have the ability to guide and control your outcomes. You are a businessperson working with businesspeople. Look for ways to encourage and inspire your clients. Display confidence in your ability to manage the project and help them achieve their goals. Serve them in such a way that you elevate them to new levels. Another timeless principle: Help others and you will be helped. Serve others well, and you will be well-served. Give, and it will be given back to you.

In summary, influence is not something you grab hold of. You cannot influence through coercion and build yourself at the same time. Influence is something you build moment-by-moment in relationships, earning the right to speak and advise.

If you want to lead, you need followers. Good leaders influence their followers by helping them, listening, encouraging, providing assistance, and solving their problems. Be a good example and you will attract followers who will bring others with them. Follow Jesus' example from his declaration recorded in MATTHEW 20:28, MARK 10:45, AND JOHN 20:28 — "*... the Son of Man did not come to be served, but to serve ...*" Leadership is service, and we serve our clients with our wisdom, knowledge, and skill.

CHAPTER THIRTY-ONE

CRAFTING YOUR PORTFOLIO

Your portfolio is your primary tool for attracting clients.

The portfolio is your most important marketing tool and is valued far more than a resumé for attracting prospective clients. Building an effective portfolio can significantly impact a your ability to acquire your ideal clients. Even if you're self-taught (you didn't go to design school) attention to your portfolio is crucial. You cannot compete as a creative professional without one.

YOUR PORTFOLIO IS NOT A SHOWCASE

Especially when establishing themselves, freelance creatives cull together various pieces to showcase their range or their interests. I've reviewed professional portfolios that included student projects from foundation courses like design theory, figure drawing, and color. This is not a good strategy for a professional portfolio. Don't treat your portfolio as if it's a showcase of your creative development or gallery of your creative work. It should be a *carefully created collection of your best work* so that viewers can assess your capabilities and fitness for their business needs. Remember, you're a creative professional who solves business problems. Your portfolio needs to communicate your ability to satisfy the needs of your target audience with a high degree of craft and creative vision.

The purpose of your portfolio is to present the type of work you *want* to do, not to showcase a random assortment of past work. Don't treat it as if it's an art exhibit of your work. Make it about the kind of work you want to get and the kinds of clients you want to serve.

This means that you need to be strategic and ruthless with what you include and why. A piece that is your favorite work may not be suitable for your portfolio because it does not address the needs of your prospective clients. When you're deciding what to include in your portfolio, ask the question, "Why am I including this?" If it's simply because you like it, omit it. Make a print of it, frame it, and hang it on your wall. If it's because you like it *and* it solves a problem, then you can include it.

IMPLEMENT A PORTFOLIO STRATEGY

Devise a strategy for your portfolio and include it in your marketing plan. Select your best work, organize it logically and according to the universal design principles of recency and hierarchy, and present it with a clear context and narrative. The rule of thumb to apply to your editing process is this: **Present the type of work you want to do, keep serial positioning in mind, and present only your best work.** Consider quantity of work, targeting your audiences, quality of work, and sequencing.

Quantity. More isn't better. The more pieces you include the more likely you'll include weak work. Limit your portfolio to 12–15 high quality, effective pieces that represent your ability to communicate and/or solve a problem. If you don't have at least 12 high quality pieces, you can include fewer. It's better to have five exemplary pieces than twenty of varying quality.

Targeting. The work you include should represent the type of projects you want to work on. For example, say you illustrate children's books, and you also earn income creating pet portraits for commission clients. That's two very different markets. Don't include the portrait work in your children's book portfolio or it will confuse your prospective clients. You need two different portfolios.

Quality. Look at your portfolio from the client's point of view and avoid sentimentality when selecting work to include. Your potential clients are simply looking for someone to help them solve a problem or communicate a message. If you consider your work in this way, you will be better able to delete the weaker pieces that devalue your overall work. Be brutally honest when judging your work. Ideally, your portfolio will contain only your most effective, highest quality, work.

Sequencing. When viewing or reading a sequence of things, people remember the first and last things in the sequence better than what's in between. Therefore, begin and end your portfolio with your strongest work. You want to tell a story about what you do, who you do it for, and why you do it.

The opening images in a portfolio create the expectation of how the rest of the portfolio will flow. When I'm reviewing a portfolio, the first two or three images presented tell me what to expect of and how to interpret the rest of the images in the book. You should open with a strong piece, position a strong piece in the middle, and close with a strong piece — sort of a "mountain and valley" sequencing. The closing image must leave a strong, memorable impression. Place your best work at the beginning, the middle and the end. Position your weaker work between these peaks.

ALWAYS BE UPDATING

Never consider your portfolio to be a finished work. Update it with your latest and greatest on a regular basis, at minimum twice a year, or as you complete client projects, keeping in mind the types of projects you're seeking, not necessarily what you've done in the past.

TELL A STORY

It's important that your portfolio communicates your unique approach to creative problem-solving. You should have a point of view. That means that your book should be cohesive. You want it to narrate how you developed an assignment from beginning to end, and how a solution addressed a specific need, purpose or problem.

This does not mean that all the work needs to be the same. It's more about all the work fitting together to convey your point of view. When your book is consistent in approach, prospective clients will have the confidence that you are able to apply that consistency to their projects. Clients will know what they can expect from you.

VERSION YOUR PORTFOLIO

A physical portfolio book is no longer required, except in certain industries. Digital options have replaced the printed portfolio — the book — but you must consider how to present your work most effectively to your prospective clients.

Versioning has two meanings. It means that you develop and maintain different *formats* of your portfolio to deploy in different environments. These can include PDFs, pitch decks, reels, website, brochures, posters, leave-behinds, etc. Versioning also refers to the ability to edit on the fly — to switch out various pieces to suit the prospective client.

Your portfolio should be editable. When you meet with a prospective client in person or on a conference call, you need to target that portfolio towards the particular prospect. Editing your portfolio to fit a specific prospective client means that you need to research your prospective client. You need to know what their business sector is, and also if they use what you create.

SHOW YOUR PROCESS

Your portfolio website should not only display your work but show your process. For certain assignments, you will want to include some preliminary work to communicate how you arrived at those solutions. Illustrators may want to show thumbnails, composition roughs and character sketches, research and color explorations. Designers may want to include concept sketches and iterations for logo development projects. Photographers may want to include screen captures of their imaging process, studio and location scenes, or the original photos used in a composited image.

Showing your process adds authority that you are the creator of the work you show and that what you show addressed a given problem or need. Showing your process reveals how you think. In response to the growth of artificial intelligence and the shortcuts people take with creative work through the use of templates and even stock images, demonstrating your process keeps the human factor intact, and the resulting work is trustworthy. It also can be legally protected by you or your client by copyright and/or trademark registration.

DIVIDE AND CONQUER

If you work in several styles or genres, divide your work into multiple portfolios. This allows you to target a specific client, subject matter, or graphic environment. For example, if you offer hand-lettering and calligraphy, illustration, and photography, you'll need three distinct portfolios because the target clientele for each is different. If you do both children's book illustration and book design, separate the work into 2 different books. You can show one or the other, or both and won't confuse your prospects by taking a "junk drawer" approach.

I had this problem as an illustrator and graphic designer. I do both, and often in combination. I started out with a single website and there split my work into different categories. Both illustration and design prospects came to my site but often were confused about what I actually do. And it was a marketing nightmare to send both audiences to one URL. I solved that problem by separating my work into two separate websites that are linked to each other. I promote them separately.

Another approach you might, and one I'm implementing currently is to position as a creative agency rather than as a individual artist. Lead with your approach and problem-solving on your home page, and link to various work portfolios that are housed on other pages in the site.

I also split social media platforms, using separate Instagram accounts for illustration and design. I promote Freelance Road Trip on X. I use LinkedIn for design and branding thought leadership and showcasing case studies. With each platform I focus on a different segment of my audience.

DEVELOP YOUR PORTFOLIO

Your portfolio is never a finished, completed work. You should have a marketing plan. The hero of that plan is your portfolio. Whenever you have downtime between client-initiated projects, work on self-initiated projects to attract the attention of your ideal clients. **Create work that will get you work**. New work should be in constant development to replace older, outdated pieces.

There is no shame in including self-assigned projects in your portfolio. Develop work that appears to solve specific visual communications problems and by which you can show some of your creative process. Think up a fictitious business or organization and design a logo for it. Then design a standards manual, a website wire frame, and a collateral brochure. If you are an illustrator and want to create children's books, develop a short series of sequential images that tell a story. If you're a photographer focusing on architecture, shoot images specifically for your portfolio that represent your point of view and the types of structures you enjoy photographing.

Be strategic about what you present in your portfolio. Include only your most effective work, and the kind of work you want to get more of. Dedicate regular blocks of time in your work to focus on portfolio development and marketing activities. If your portfolio is not consistently strong or is confusing, your marketing efforts won't be as effective and you'd like them to be.

YOUR PORTFOLIO IS YOUR PRIMARY MARKETING TOOL

I've never been asked by a client to show my resumé. You won't be asked for one, either, unless you're seeking employment. Your portfolio is your primary means of attracting clients. Instead of working on a resumé, put that time and effort into your body of work. Include pieces that are distinctively your style, that demonstrate your ability to creatively solve business problems, and that represent your creative approach, reliability, and vision.

TAKE ACTION

Something you can do immediately to improve your portfolio is to objectively review and edit your work. Put yourself in the position of an art buyer, editor, or prospective client. Avoid relying on personal preferences.

If you have more than twelve pieces, remove the weakest and anything you're not sure about.

Remove any work you included because it's your favorite, because the portfolio is not about you. Its purpose is to demonstrate how you solve visual communications problems for clients. If you have a strong emotional connection to a piece you may not be seeing it the way a client would.

Is your portfolio consistent in style and approach? If your book appears to include the work of several different creatives it will not be effective in achieving your business goals. Variety is a good thing but too much of it results in chaos which will confuse your prospects. Remove the inconsistent pieces.

CHAPTER THIRTY-TWO

ESSENTIALS FOR YOUR WEBSITE

The intersection of sound aesthetics, creative problem-solving, and legal compliance.

I shared earlier the necessity and benefits of having your own website under your own domain. While I advocate for designing and maintaining your own on shared hosting platforms, managed hosting platforms are very popular for their ease of use. Whether your site is housed on managed hosting, shared servers, or your own server, there are specific legal requirements you need to pay attention to and implement. This chapter is a compendium of content and features you're required to include on your website in addition to your portfolio and contact information. These are not listed in any order.

Cookie notice. All websites use cookies which are bits of data stored by your web browser so that your device is recognized and information from previous visits — login credentials, user preferences, and more. Cookies are either essential or non-essential. There are first-party cookies and third-party cookies. Visitors to your site should be able to give their permission — their consent — before storing or accessing cookies on their device.

Your website must have a cookie notice so that users are informed about what cookies are used, why they are used (e.g., for analytics, marketing), and what data is collected. They should have the ability to accept some or all cookies, or to reject them, and to easily change their preferences. Cookie notices commonly appear at the bottom of a browser window or as a pop-up that appears when a visitor clicks a link or scrolls. In short, your website should comply with data privacy laws such as the GDPR (General Data Protection Regulation) and the CCPA (California Consumer Privacy Act), both of which have specific requirements for cookie consent.

Privacy Policy. The cookie consent notice must link to your website's privacy policy which is a page that explains how your site uses cookies.

Copyright notice. Your website footer should include a copyright notice, usually in this format: ©year date, your name or business name if you're claiming copyright as your business. Designated all rights reserved or all international rights reserved. Additionally, copyright notice should be included on your Terms of Use page. Display of a copyright notice does not equate to legally registering copyright. See Chapter xx .

Terms of Use. This page explains what is permitted for the visitor when using your website, and what's prohibited. For example, right-clicking can be prohibited. AI training can be prohibited. Keep in mind that prohibition doesn't equate to inability. You should state in writing what is permitted and what is prohibited for visitors on your site, but enforcement requires your direct attention.

If you sell products or digital downloads on your website, include a customer service contact number and email, mailing address, and refund policy. If you offer a guarantee, that should also be described in detail on the Terms of use Page.

If you include a mailing list subscription link, the Terms of Use should include how to unsubscribe.

Accessibility. Lawsuits are increasing around ease of use for those needing special accommodations. Performance standards now center around website content and features being perceivable, audible, understandable, and robust. Deployment of sound design principles If your website is housed on a managed hosting platform, basic accessibility should be included, but you may need to enhance it. If your site is built on a framework like Wordpress or from code and script, you'll either format the code or install a plugin to ensure your site is accessible. At minimum, be sure your textual copy, links, and color scheme provide enough value contrast and are set for readability. Every image should include **"alt text" descriptives** which convey the content of an image in text form. Alt text can be configured in the image metadata or added in the website's back end. **Videos should include captions** or a transcript should be provided so that the hearing-impaired can understand the information. **Form input fields should be labeled**. Background and text color should have enough **value contrast** to accommodate color-blind visitors. So that screen readers can differentiate between sections, **text should be coded using semantic markup** (<header> <footer> <H2>.) The ability to **navigate the site via keyboard only** is also required. These are a few of the minimum accessibility requirements.

Although your website most likely does not exist for the purpose of offering programs and benefits to the public, if you include a mailing list subscription option or contact form, accessibility requirements will apply. The ADA (Americans With Disabilities Act) requires that businesses serving the public (that includes you), businesses of 15 or more employees, and government agencies ensure their websites are accessible.

Finally, your site should be **responsive,** meaning that it can be viewed at a variety of screen dimensions and resolutions.

You may not think that your business serves the public in the way a restaurant or medical practice does, but consider that, by implementing accessibility standards, your site's search engine optimization (SEO) is enhanced and you build reputation for being committed to inclusive design. Be cautious about thinking that the requirements don't apply to your freelance business. They will apply if you design websites and apps for clients. *The prudent sees danger and hides himself, but the simple go on and suffer for it.* — PROVERBS 22:3 ESV.

FRONT-FACING CONTENT

Essential content for your website:

Your portfolio: still images, videos, reels.

Your about page describing your approach, history, and point of view. You can also include your client roster here.

Your contact information.

Terms of use pertaining to how visitors may use your website

Privacy policy, including how your site conforms to legal requirements.

Supplemental content to include if you desire:

Case studies

Client testimonials (enhances social proof)

Blog

Newsletter sign-up form connected to an email service.

Merchandise store

When crafting your website maintain its purpose as a marketing tool in mind. It's not an online art gallery. It's your primary presence on the internet, and your home base for all your marketing and promotion efforts.

CHAPTER THIRTY-THREE

CRAFTING YOUR BRAND

What are you known for?

Next to your portfolio, your brand is the most important factor when it comes to attracting clients. Your brand represents your business and is conveyed in your visual brand, your reputation, your positioning and differentiation among other creatives, your service offerings, and who you serve. All aspects of your brand intertwine into a total narrative that identifies and promotes your business and your unique creative work.

Many freelance creatives, including myself, are **brand designers** and strategists who help shape the brands of their clients. **Brand** is defined as *a person's perception of a product, service, experience, or organization.* **Brand identity** is the *visual expression* of a brand. Your logo is not your brand. As a freelancer, you are your brand, and when you engage in the intentional, purposeful development of your brand you address both its professional and personal aspects. Every interaction you have with colleagues and with clients and prospects on social media platforms, in email, on your website, and in person, helps to build your brand and establish your reputation in the marketplace.

WHY BRANDING IS CRUCIAL

Branding is crucial simply because of the amount of options available to businesses and organizations in selecting creative talent to work with. Every business and organization has to battle for territory in the minds and hearts of their target audiences, and to be memorable and remarkable requires thought and focused action. Brands are shortcuts through the myriad choices available in the marketplace. They're a beacon of light shining out from the masses of sameness. A client looking to develop a brand will more likely work with a creative who is branded than one who's not. As previously stated, after your portfolio, branding should be your primary focus if you want to succeed in business.

Branding enables you to compete on your own terms. When you brand, you don't have to compete on pricing, discounts or package deals. Instead, you make yourself attractive to your best kind of client. Branding serves as a filter that turns away those who aren't ideal. Branding gives you the ability to say no: "I'm sorry, but that's not what I do."

A thoughtfully crafted visual brand speaks volumes about your target market, your style, and your areas of expertise.

WHAT IS BRANDING?

If you have a logo and a web site, you have not created your brand. These and other visual assets are the means by which you connect with others. They are *representations* of your brand, but are not in and of themselves your brand.

Brand is *reputation*. It's what others think of you. Brands are not actually designed but are built on the opinions and trust of the marketplace. Everything we do in business either supports or tears down our reputation — from the type of work we do to the types of clients we work with.

In the brand development process, we create graphic assets that uniquely identify, position and differentiate our work from that of others. We communicate not just what we do but how we do it. We develop copy and visuals that explain why a client should work with us as opposed to someone else.

We compete for share of mind, for recognition and the acknowledgment of others. When developing a brand, we answer: Who am I? Who needs to know? Why do they need to know? How will they find out? How do I want them to respond?

Branding involves making your work and services not just available but relevant to your audience which consists of those prospects you can serve well and want to work with. How do you want your freelance business to be perceived, and how can you shape that image? What do you want to be known for? Without a brand, your approach will lack clarity. When things are confusing or obtuse, people won't trust them.

Brand is a promise to the clients we serve. They're relational. They're ideas. You should notice that people attach to brands, trust them, promote them, identify with them, and develop strong loyalties to them. Consider the brands you love and why you love them. Brands that are crafted well and keep the customer in mind help build successful businesses, while ineffective brands actually counteract success.

BRAND FIRST, THEN PROMOTE

Generally, once freelancers have a curated portfolio of work, they are prone to launch directly into marketing and promotion. In doing so they overlook a crucial step which is to determine how they should be perceived in the marketplace. No one can offer something (creative services, for instance) without knowing what it is and why it's necessary. Knowing what it is and what the need is leads to knowing how to communicate it.

Without a solid brand and strategy for implementation, your marketing efforts won't be wholly effective. Anyone who sells goods to customers or services to clients needs to take branding seriously if they are profit-minded.

THE BASIS OF YOUR BRAND

Your brand should be honest and relevant in order to invite the right people to connect with you. As an independent creative professional, branding must be both professional and personal. You brand your business, but you're the front face of your business. Therefore your branding needs to consider your whole reputation — you personally as the founder/owner of your business, as well as your business itself. Your brand needs to be authentically you, but not casual, off-the-cuff you. Your goal is to strategically communicate your expertise, values, and personality in order to build a strong, positive, and memorable impression in both professional and personal spheres. Developing your brand has to be careful and intentional. You have to influence public perception by way of appearance, authority, authenticity, and audience.

A BRANDING FRAMEWORK FOR FREELANCE CREATIVES

Brand development can be broken down into four pillars:

1. Purpose and mission (authenticity)
2. Visual (graphic) assets (appearance)
3. Message (authority)
4. Target audience/prospective clients (audience)

Purpose: You have to get clear about what you do, and why it's relevant. This process should not be overlooked, and requires some soul-searching. Why is freelancing so important to you? Why not just get a job? What do you really do: paint pretty pictures for kids' books or help young readers understand values and how the world works? Successful brands are deeply rooted in purpose and values. Take time to thoughtfully consider the transformational aspects of your creative work — transformational not for you but for your clients.

Appearance: Your approach, position, and differentiation, even your secret sauce, are expressed in the visual designs you create to communicate your brand. Is your persona more of a helper or a guide? Are you a global thinker or more detail oriented? Are you a wise counselor or a free-thinking outlaw? Is your customer base refined and serious or rowdy and adventurous?

Authenticity is how you share your message with the world. It includes social media, list-building, advertising, direct mail, email and networking, to start with. It's through your marketing channels that you become known, recognized, and trusted. Therefore consistency in message, look and feel, and frequency is important.

Audience is who you're addressing. The whole world isn't your audience. Your ideal client isn't everyone. Your audience is a small segment of a large population. Audience also includes your current and past clients. Branding needs to be maintained within the working relationship. Integrity is necessary. Are you consistent with your brand while working with clients? Keep in mind that clients will recommend you or not depending on how you treat them.

BRAND IS RELATIONSHIP

The purpose of branding is to build awareness that leads to working relationships. It's a long-term commitment that becomes fruitful over time. Manage your own expectations and be patient and tenacious. When prospects enjoy repeated positive and meaningful encounters with your brand, they open up more easily to the idea of working with you. People prefer to work with people they know, like, and trust. Commit to developing a visual brand and strategy for implementation, then follow through with your plan, and stick with it for the long haul. Don't give up if response is minimal at first. Keep going.

CHAPTER THIRTY-FOUR

ATTRACTING THE RIGHT CLIENTS

The value of a client profile

If you want to attract the kinds of clients you're best suited to serve, you have to recognize them. To recognize them you first need to describe them. This is called profiling. Without a preferred client profile, commonly called a *buyer persona*, you have no filter and are likely to work with those who are not a good fit. An ideal client is one for whom you do the kind of work you want to do, who pays you to do it for them, and you get along with them well.

You cannot market your work effectively to everyone. Not everyone needs what you do. That means you will need to identify specific prospects within the larger business population that have problems you can solve. To be ideal, those prospects need creative services like yours and are willing to make the investment.

Once you have identified your ideal client type, the next step is to attract them to you. I use the concept of *attraction* rather than pursuit because it's more effective to be attractive than to chase prospects. Being attractive takes some effort on your part, but it pays off in the long run as clients seek you out because they know that you can solve their problems and assist in their success.

What follow are not specific how-tos or tips. Rather, I advocate for a point of view or *mindset* in thinking about your work and how you serve others through it. **As a freelancer you are less likely than an employee to be selected for your capabilities than for the benefits you provide.** You will not build your reputation because your vectorizing skills are incomparable, or because you can draw a photorealistic portrait of a celebrity in Procreate. Clients will work with you because they trust you. You build trust by creating effective work that solves their business problems.

DECIDE WHAT IT IS THAT YOU DO

Creatives are naturally divergent rather than convergent thinkers. We are stimulated by a lot of ideas and can become bored doing one thing repeatedly. Deciding on a niche, specializing in one thing and going deep in that, goes against our natures. We want to do so manydifferent things. The problem with this desire is that we can become dabblers with shallow knowledge of each thing we desire to do. We cannot easily become masters of multiple interests.

A sane solution is to become a *specialized generalist* by combining multiple skills in a unique way so that it becomes your competitive advantage in the marketplace. You can go deep on the combined skills, become known for it, and command higher fees. Combine your creative and marketing skills, for example. Or combine lifestyle photography with packaging design.

Another solution is to maintain a broad skill set, but position as an agency. As a company of one, I position as a consultancy with a brand strategy and design focus. This allows me to combine several different skills necessary for brand development.

Still another niche option is to specialize in a specific industry or type of client. You might position on developing marketing materials for veterinarians, for example. Or combine calligraphy and hand lettering with title design for film and video.

Consider what you enjoy doing and decide how to narrow your focus and niche down. What skills do you have that, if combined, can become a unique offer for prospective clients who are dealing with the kinds of problems your skills can solve? To become attractive to your ideal client,

MASTER YOUR CRAFT

Excellence is not perfection. It is the quality of being really good at what you do. One thing to consider if you want to attract your ideal clients: Be consistently outstanding. This means that you continually develop your craft and strive to improve. Don't stall out in developing your artistry, skill, and creative thinking. If you are not growing and developing, you are not maturing in your work. Study, reading, research and practice are the four pillars of becoming a *master* designer, illustrator or photographer. The same four pillars should be applied to your business knowledge. You should never stop learning.

Additionally, you should never send anything out the door that is not of the highest quality in creative problem-solving and craftsmanship. By creating excellent work you are more likely to attract an excellent clientele. Do mediocre work, and you will attract clients of that quality.

Here's a Biblical basis for excellence in your work: *Do you see a man who excels in his work? He will stand before kings; He will not stand before unknown men.* PROVERBS 22:29 NKJV. I like how it's expressed in the not-so-new King James Version: *Seest thou a man diligent in his business? He shall stand before kings; he shall not stand before mean men.*

Here's the conclusion: To freelance well you have to attract clients. To attract the right clients you have to offer relevant solutions, and be excellent in your craft and in how you do business.

SOLVE REAL PROBLEMS

Be the solution provider your clients want to work with. They have needs and problems that you should be able to address. This means that, once you've identified your client base, you then find out through research, networking and asking questions what their problems are that you can solve. For example, I met a fellow business owner at a conference who, upon learning that I am a graphic designer, mentioned that her firm had worked with a number of designers who were difficult in one way or another. Some promised more than they could deliver. Another could not stay on budget. A couple of others seemed to be distracted. These are real problems that cause clients to throw up their hands. How would you be able to address these kinds of problems? How would you position your freelance business in a way that eliminates these real concerns?

CONNECT CONSISTENTLY

In your outreach planning (your marketing plan) what methods will you use to connect with your ideal prospects? Will you attend networking events and conferences? Will you use social media and streaming? Will you create a newsletter? Will you join chambers of commerce? Become a speaker? Will you produce behind-the-scenes or reaction videos?

Devise a plan, add everything to your calendar with due dates, and set alerts as reminders. Then, follow through on what you've scheduled. You will not gain a client by sending one promotion piece, or by posting a few times. Long term consistency builds awareness and reminds people who you are and what you do.

At the same time, don't over-commit. When you spread your marketing efforts too broadly, you will have trouble keeping up. Narrow your focus based on your ideal client profile. A small, curated audience will yield better results than a large, unfocused list. One of my colleagues — a surface designer and calligrapher — invested many hours into creating a one-of-a-kind self-promotion box targeted to one well-known celebrity designer she wanted to work with. In creating that piece, she researched the designer's work and customers, created a collection of original, style-aligned designs, wrote a hand-written cover letter, and sent everything off to the designer. She was able to connect and worked with the designer on several lucrative high-profile projects. This is a real life example of the benefits of knowing who your ideal client is and going above and beyond to attract them.

FOCUS ON BENEFITS

By promoting your skills you'll attract prospective clients who will treat you as a wrist and not as a creative partner. If your marketing focus is on how clients *benefit*, you will be more attractive. Therefore, focus on results and outcomes. How will they be transformed by working with you? Change the descriptions on your web site and promotional pieces to describe what clients gain when working with you. How do you solve their marketing, branding and visual communications problems? How can you help them achieve their business objectives?

A results focus shifts you from pursuing to attracting the clients you want to work with. Making this kind of shift requires you to think differently about your work and why you do it. What kinds of clients, industries, or companies do you want to work with? What benefits do you provide your clients? What do you help them accomplish? With what kinds of project budgets do you seek? Get started by writing a short descriptive statement following this format:

> For [*describe your ideal client and industry*] I create [*describe your primary service offering*] so that they can [*describe one or two benefits or results you make possible*].
>
> Example: *I develop brand strategy and visual designs for purpose-driven enterprises so they can achieve their business goals.*

Don't rush through this little exercise. Give it some serious thought based on what you want to do and who you want to serve through what you do.

CHAPTER THIRTY-FIVE

YOUR IDEAL CLIENT STRATEGY

You're not just working on a project together, you're in a relationship.

In the previous chapter we covered what to do to make yourself attractive to prospective clients. In this chapter we're discussing how to identify the types of clients you're best suited to serve. Good clients are integral to successful freelance projects and to your career overall. Beyond the project work itself, a referral or recommendation from the right client can open doors for you. But how do you choose good clients? How do you know up front that a prospect will be okay to work with? How do you recognize what a good client is?

CREATE A "GOOD CLIENT" STRATEGY

To weed out undesirables (and they are out there), you need to be intentional and strategic. When you're working with clients, you're not just working on a project, you're in a relationship. Setting high standards for those relationships begins during your prospecting for clients before you agree to work together. Don't wait until you've started the project to start relating.

The point is to value the working relationship and your own peace of mind enough to be willing to pass on less desirable situations so that you can do your best work in the best way possible for the best clients. There are various ways to filter your prospects. I have these suggestions for qualifying clients to weed out those you want to work with. You may want to add your own criteria to fit your unique situation.

Look for clients **you will enjoy working with**. Just as you have preferences in choosing friends, apply those preferences when selecting your clients.

Look for clients **who understand that you are a business owner,** and expect you to make your living from your business, and are comfortable with paying you for your time and effort on their behalf.

Look for clients **who understand what you do**, and who have worked with a professional designer, illustrator, photographer or writer previously. Try to avoid being the one to break them in. You do now want to be a client's first experience working with a freelance creative.

Seek clients who are **willing to discuss their project up front**, including giving you a budget to work with. Some prospects are cryptic and fearful of divulging information and of signing contracts. You cannot determine whether you should take on the work if you don't know enough about it to decide. Walk away from those who are not open with you.

Look for clients who are **willing to sign a contract and provide a down payment** before you begin the work. This shows good faith on their part, and give you the ability to begin the project funded.

Look for clients **who will designate one representative to work with you**. Larger clients and organizations may have a board or group overseeing the project on their end. Require that they designate a single decision maker bestowed with the ability to made decisions. This may be a marketing director, art buyer, editor, executive director. Designing for a committee is unproductive and drains your resources because everyone will have a different opinion and want to share it.

Seek clients **who are the right size for your business**. You don't want a single client to be a huge proportion of your overall income, and you don't want one so small that you become their lifeline. Look for clients who are not so big that, if you lose them, you will be severely impacted financially. Smaller clients are known to be more needy and will seek you out and depend on you for more than what you've contracted for.

Look for clients **who will respect your boundaries**. Some will attempt to re-define your role, asking for favors or services that are not what you would normally provide.

Seek clients **who will treat you as a professional peer**, not a hireling. As a freelancer, you come alongside your clients and partner with them but don't work *for* them. You should have a peer-to-peer relationship rather than a boss-employee relationship. Along these line, be careful of the words you use. Saying you're working *for* a client indicates you're an employee. Instead, say you're working *with* a client.

CREATE A STRATEGY THAT WORKS FOR YOU.

Remember that freelancing is about freedom and choices. When you accept business relationships that become a burden, you are no longer free. Only you can determine what a good client means for you. Taking the time to qualify prospective clients up front is one of the best investments you will make.

CHAPTER THIRTY-SIX

SELF-PROMOTION

Freelancers should always be marketing.

Self promotion is the practice of telling potential clients about what you do. With it you build your brand, engage prospects and find clients. Self promotion involves making yourself known through a distinct online presence, showcasing your work, networking both online and in person, and consistently connecting with your audience.

SELF-PROMOTION AND MARKETING

Self-promotion is a sub-category of marketing. Marketing is a broad category of activities that includes advertising, public relations, self-promotion, content creation, networking, sponsorships, social media engagement, and others. Marketing, including self-promotion, should be a top priority if you desire to have a consistent stream of work. Self promotion can be defined as marketing for the individual — yourself. As a freelancer you need to create a marketing plan with a self-promotion focus — the things you personally can do to connect with and communicate to your most suitable client base. When you serve a clientele, you're promoting yourself. When you create and sell products, you're marketing your products. That's the simplest way to describe the difference between the two concepts.

SELF-PROMOTION AND BRANDING

Where self-promotion centers on activities that grow your business, branding is the development of unique communications created to build your reputation in the marketplace. Marketing is a communication process. Branding is founded on mission, divine calling (life purpose), values, persona, differentiation, and competitive advantage among other aspects, with the purpose of managing perceptions. Marketing uses branding to achieve business objectives.

Branding is the compass for your marketing efforts. You should want to develop a unique, consistent, and authentic brand, and then use marketing tactics to become known and build influence.

HOW TO USE SELF-PROMOTION

As a low or no cost means of sharing your message, promotion can be undertaken in a variety of ways. A newsletter, new project announcements, new services, relevant insights, and holiday greetings are all good fodder and reasons for self-promotion. Plan campaigns that target segments of your market.

It's necessary to define your *ideal clients* and then create a marketing plan to target them consistently. If you desire to develop business within a particular market sector, for example, functional health or extreme sports, you'll need to research those markets to determine who uses the creative services you offer. Build a contact list, and begin sending your branded promotions. A *contact list* is essential to your marketing strategy, and so is keeping it updated regularly — at least twice a year. People move around a lot. Targeted lists can be purchased, and you can also develop a list on your own from your networking. Ask for referrals from current clients and colleagues to help flesh out your list. Let people who know you know you're in business and seeking clients.

Freelance creatives should always be marketing, even with project deadlines. Batch create your promotions for an entire year, for a quarter, or for a month, in advance, and schedule them to automatically publish in your email client and on your social platforms. Automating your marketing helps you remain top of mind with existing and prospective clients, and minimized effort on your part.

BEGIN WITH YOUR WEB SITE

Your most important tool for self promotion is your web site, which we addressed in regard to content in a previous chapter. It is the home base and hub for all of your marketing. Owning your own real estate under your own domain to showcase your portfolio, present your working philosophy, accomplishments, and point of view is an absolute must. Not having a web site under your own branded domain reduces your legitimacy in the business world.

All your marketing channels should lead back to your website. It's the only platform you own and fully control. It functions as a stable, centralized hub where all traffic, offers, and messaging ultimately lead. Every campaign you launch — email, social, advertising, podcasting, or public relations — should point to a conversion-focused destination that you manage. When you build your website with marketing strategy in mind, it functions as the point of engagement, trust, and business growth.

PORTFOLIO DIRECTORIES

A secondary tool for self promotion is a portfolio or directory platform. Examples of these platforms include Behance, Creative Hotlist, Dripbook, and Dribbble. Many charge an annual fee or subscription. A few are by invitation only. These are not your own real estate, so the idea is to use them to expand your influence and social proof. As with your social media and email marketing, they should lead people back to your own website. Always strive to get people onto your own web site.

CREATIVE SERVICES DIRECTORIES

Creative services directories are showcases where designers, illustrators, and photographers buy ad space in print and online editions, and have access to database lists of art buyers, creative directors, publishers, design firms and ad agencies. They're viable options to increase visibility, build credibility, and attract potential clients. Directory listings can be searched by region, job title, type of work, and industry. Examples of creative directories include the Directory of Illustration and Workbook Creative, Inc.

LOCAL BUSINESS LISTINGS

Business listings are online directories where you can create a profile with your contact information and link your website. Yelp is a well-known example of this. Your local chamber of commerce will include business listings on its website. Bare bones listings on these platforms are usually free. Enhanced, branded listings and advertising are paid options.

A key to utilizing business listings effectively is to know who your ideal audience is and where they look for the services you offer. If they don't look for creative service providers on Yelp, that platform won't be worth your effort. Research to learn what is best for you to use. Some of the best known listing services are:

Yelp listings are a standard for businesses and customer reviews.

Manta focuses on small businesses and entrepreneurs.

ZoomInfo is a business-to-business (B2B) service that gathers data on businesses, owners, and industries from around the internet with a focus on lead generation.

A **Google Business Profile** can increase the likelihood of prospective clients finding you because of increased visibility in search results and traffic to your website.

Because they're not targeted toward your ideal client profile, local business listings can prove to be an ineffective means for building awareness. The majority of users of these sites are consumers looking for what's available in their neighborhoods and communities. Always keep your ideal client profile in mind when choosing self-promotion options.

CROWDSOURCING PLATFORMS

Crowdsourcing platforms exist in a variety of formats. Those seeking to match freelancers with prospective clients can be viable sources of projects and revenue, but they can also be a waste of time and money. Platforms such as Fiverr, 99designs, Upwork, and Freelancer provide independent contractors with opportunities to create a profile and to search for potential projects. Prospective clients seeking freelance talent post opportunities for freelancers to bid on.

Platforms such as TopTal and PeoplePerHour are dedicated to showcasing freelancers in particular industries or areas of expertise such as marketing or coding.

Challenges you might experience in using crowdsourcing platforms include the inability to target your prospects, the amount of competition on the platforms, and competing for projects based on price alone, with projects often awarded to the lowest bidders. There are also the service fees and membership fees. While these fees are tax-deductible business expenses, they reduce the amount of profit you generate on a project.

With a solid strategy and consistent effort it's possible to make a living through crowdsourcing, but do your homework to find the best option(s) for the kind of work you do and the types of clients you seek. Research the platforms to compare success rates and project opportunities. As I previously advised, always keep your ideal client profile in mind when choosing self-promotion options, and do the work to establish yourself once you make your choice.

EMAIL AND DIRECT MAIL

Put your work directly in front of potential buyers and clients on a regular basis to let them know what you offer by targeting. The most effective means for this it targeting, which employs taking direct aim at a narrow, well-defined prospect pool.

Targeting usually involves an offensive (meaning pro-active) strategy of email marketing and list building. Email campaigns sent via services such as Mailchimp and Constant Contact remain the most effective means of self-promotion. Why? Because you build a list of contacts that want to hear from you. They give you permission to connect when they join your mailing list.

In return for their permission to contact them, you give them relevant content which can be promotions of your work, newsletters, announcements, behind-the-scenes (BTS) videos and stills, articles, and insights.

Your contacts should be thoughtfully curated, which means research is necessary. Don't simply toss random names onto a list, or buy a list and send the same promotion to everyone on it. Match contacts to the type of work you do, and categorize (segment) your contacts according to interest or industry. If you're an illustrator targeting ad agencies, you should not include agencies on your list that buy only photography. Pick and choose your contacts based on how appropriate your work is to them. To do this, look at the current work on their web sites.

With email you can personalize your messages by segmenting, targeting, and tracking opens and click through rates (CTR). Email marketing strategies that use persuasive language, engaging imagery, intriguing subject lines, and appealing calls to action are more likely to succeed. As with social media content, consistency over time is necessary for becoming known and landing clients. And because it's permission-based, email marketing provides a higher return on investment than other marketing activities.

Direct mail is the process of creating and sending physical, printed promotions to a targeted audience. Postcards, brochures, and letters are examples of direct mail marketing. Because of the costs of printing, postage, and mailing, direct mail requires a greater material investment, but historically it yields a high return compared to other self-promotion methods.

One benefit of using direct mail is that, at the very least, the recipient has to handle the piece to look at it, assess its merits, and then decide what to do with it. It cannot be immediately deleted without some sort of physical interaction. Direct mail was previously the preferred way of getting one's work in front of prospective clients. Because of the lock-downs in 2020–2023, many people worked from home and still do, so direct mail has become less effective in reaching specific people.

Direct mail can integrate with email and be used to send people to your website and subscribe to your newsletter if you include a QR code that links to your website, blog, or a landing page.

In regard to QR codes, if you carry **business cards**, consider them as physical promotion pieces and include a QR code so that prospects can connect directly with your website. In many industries and professions business cards are still considered necessary for networking, building a contact list, and doing business in general.

Mailing lists of professional roles, regions, and industries can be purchased or acquired through annual subscriptions. You want to make sure you're receiving good value for what you're paying, and that the lists are current and in compliance with current privacy and spam laws. The safest way to build a list is through consent, with opt-in features on your website, so be circumspect when purchasing lists. It's more effective to have a small list of engaged recipients than a large list of disinterested contacts. Even if your list is has only 15 contacts on it and one of them is your mother, start sending promotions. Start small. Grow big.

NETWORKING

Even if you're an introvert, networking is an excellent means of building your contact list and acquiring projects. Join business networking groups, your local chamber of commerce, and service clubs, and get to know people on a face-to-face basis. Work on community projects and events with them. Because people prefer to work with people they know, trust, and like, building basic human relationships helps you build your influence and reputation. Don't overlook the opportunities these organizations present to you.

PROMOTING ON SOCIAL MEDIA

Use your social media platforms to increase your visibility and connect with a broader audience. Social media marketing is generally low-cost compared to other marketing options, and helps increase your search visibility. Set up business or creator profiles on LinkedIn and other social platforms that your prospective clients use. Build a curated list of hashtags and key phrases and use it consistently across all your platforms. Post your own content on a regular basis, and be sure to interact with prospects on the platform by commenting and reacting to their posts.

A key understanding to adopt when using social media is to stay current with changes to algorithms, which change frequently. What worked for reaching your audience last week won't work next week. It's necessary to keep watch and adjust quickly.

UTILIZING CURRENT AND PAST CLIENTS

Your current and previous clients can be excellent sources for new clients and projects. Ask for referrals and communicate your availability for new work. If you've done excellent, effective work for them, you have a firm basis for asking.

Word to the wise: When you do excellent work and provide a professional experience, your clients are more likely to refer you. But you do have to ask, because once a project is completed they will move on quickly and won't generally be aware that you're looking for new work.

UTILIZING FRIENDS AND FAMILY

Among your colleagues, friends, and family are referral opportunities. The people you know are acquainted with people who need your services. Utilize your acquaintances and family members to find new freelance opportunities. Just ask them: “Hey, I’ve just started my freelance business. Is there someone you’ve done business with who could use my services?” or “I’m currently accepting new projects. I’d love to connect with Amazing Company, and I know that the owner is a member of the same Toastmasters group you are. Can I take you both out for coffee?”

Word to the wise: When asking friends and family be very specific about what you are looking for. On occasion I’ve mentioned to friends that I’m looking for new clients and have gotten responses along the lines of, ”Oh! I know The Home Depot is hiring. I saw a sign on their door,” and, “My neighbor is looking to renovate their kitchen. I’ll give them your phone number.” Understand that your close connections and friends may not really understand what you do and who you serve, so be clear with them.

ALWAYS BE MARKETING.

Promotion and marketing are vital for building your business but are often neglected by freelance creatives. Every freelancer should consider marketing as a number one priority for keeping their project pipeline flowing steadily. It’s a building process that has to take place over years. Establish your unique brand, maintain a contact list, and create and schedule promotions on an ongoing basis. Become your own client and create content with the same level of care and intention you’d use when working with a paying client.

CHAPTER THIRTY-SEVEN

PLANNING YOUR MARKETING

Planning gives you a road map to reach your destination.

Marketing is vital for your business success. You cannot hope to succeed in your creative enterprise without marketing, and to promote your business successfully, you need a solid plan. Your marketing plan is your road map: Decide where you want to end up and map out your route before you get behind the wheel. In a sense, your marketing plan is more important than your business plan, since you cannot acquire clients and earn revenue without letting people know about you. That's the essence of marketing.

Many freelancers — and I count myself among them — do not like marketing. We find it easier to create marketing materials and content for others than for ourselves. We engage in marketing activities because we need to if we want to find clients.

MARKETING IS NOT SELLING

There is something we need to get over. Marketing is not selling. If we understand that we are always marketing on a daily basis in terms of influencing others and building our reputations, it's a quick translation to marketing our creative work.

You can't earn income if you have no clients.

To get clients, you need to attract them to you.

The activities you pursue to attract clients is called *marketing*.

WHAT IS SELLING?

Few people appreciate pushy salespeople. Selling is often considered sleazy. But it's an aspect of marketing in which you close the client or customer, meaning that they've agreed to work with you or buy from you.

The difference between marketing and selling is that selling is essentially persuasion while marketing is research, development, positioning, and reputation building. Marketing builds awareness and sales converts prospects into clients or customers. The intended result of marketing is sales.

YOU NEED A MARKETING PLAN

A marketing plan removes many of the unknowns in attracting clients. It puts you in control of when, where and how your work is seen and who will see it. Creating a plan helps you focus narrowly on the kinds of clients you want to work with so that you don't waste your efforts chasing those who aren't a good fit for you. We discussed how to create a profile of your ideal client in a previous chapter.

A marketing plan serves to solidify your hoped-for future if you put it into practice. In it you propose methods and strategies to follow through on. The plan is evidence of your profit motive and designates the amount of profit you intend to create.

A marketing plan clarifies your brand and messaging so that you don't create confusion for your prospective clients. It should include your preferred client profile and how you will find and communicate with them — your marketing channels.

A marketing plan provides a way to measure the effectiveness of your promotional efforts. You decide what you want to achieve, determine how you will achieve those things, and by when. This makes your progress measurable in that you know what you're aiming for and also know when you hit your target. You'll also know if you miss the target, and differentiate between what activities worked and what didn't, so you can adjust accordingly.

A written marketing plan makes it more likely that you will follow through and execute the plan. When you have calendared the activities you will send your email promotions, attend a networking meeting, or post new work on your website, and set reminders you are more likely to actually do the work.

A marketing plan allows you to determine a variety of activities and spread them out over specified time periods. It gives you a big-picture point of view.

A marketing plan reduces your need for referrals. While referrals and recommendations say a lot about your expertise and professionalism, relying solely or mostly on referrals means you're letting others control your workflow and your client base. That can be very risky for your business. When you create and implement a plan that includes a variety of channels and platforms, you take the wheel, driving your "vehicle" where you want it to go. You're able to choose who you work with. And, if a particular activity does not yield the desired results, you can omit or replace it and continue on with the successful channels.

And the primary reason you need a marketing plan? It reduces your risk of failing. In consistently executing your plan you should eventually notice an increase in traffic, in responses, in connections, and in influence, all of which will help attract new clients and retain existing ones. The results compound over time if you remain consistent in your efforts.

CREATE YOUR MARKETING PLAN

Marketing is effective over time if you're consistent with it. You may not see immediate results. Be reasonable in your expectations and continue to take action on your plan every week. Over time, you should start noticing a difference in your work flow and cash flow.

I stated earlier that freelancers need to always be marketing. You do this in a variety of methods:

Relationship marketing focuses on building relationships with existing and potential clients and edifying customer loyalty.

Word of mouth marketing is not something you engage in for yourself. Even so, it's a very effective aspect of marketing because it relies on what others think and say about you. When they recommend you to their colleagues and give you referrals it's because of how you've worked with them and created successful solutions for them. Word of mouth marketing can go either way — positive or negative.

Digital marketing is anything deployed via the internet, email, or social media platforms. It can be paid or not.

Paid advertising incorporates traditional marketing approaches such as TV ads, radio, podcast sponsorships, and print media.

Cause marketing connects products and services to a social cause or issue. You might help sponsor and promote a no-kill shelter adoption event, or announce that a percentage of your profits are designated for certain types of non-profit organizations.

To conclude, marketing is a significant and necessary business activity. It's essential for creating brand awareness, increasing profits, and retaining clients. It's acts as fuel for your business momentum. Without it, you cannot sustain your business for the long haul. It affects every other aspect of your business mechanics.

CHAPTER THIRTY-EIGHT

HOW TO WORK WITH CLIENTS

Best Practices For Building Reputation and Relationships

When you accept a client's project, you need to make it your own. While you're not creating for yourself, you should approach every project as if it's your money and reputation on the line.

Your role is to share your client's message with the community they are targeting on behalf of your client. To do that effectively, there are several actions you will want to incorporate into your approach to every project and client relationship:

1. Understand your client's vision. This is where your role begins. If you don't understand what your client is aiming to accomplish and the motivations that drive them, you can't create what they need. You have nothing to communicate. Getting to know the client's vision, audience and motives requires conversational and listening skills. You need to look for what is said and also what is implied. Think of implication as the auditory white space between one's words and sentences. Wrap up the conversation with, "Okay, this is what I understand your goals are..." and then summarize their key concerns.

2. Understand your client's role in their marketplace. Behind the client's vision are their purpose and position. How does the client live out their vision in their day-to-day internal operations and external relationships with their customers? Ask a lot of questions: What are they doing? What are they accomplishing by doing it? How is it going? What's missing?

3. Understand the client's customers — their audience. Don't simply look at whether the audience is primarily male or female, a certain age range, a certain location, with a certain amount of education and income level. Consider the concerns and interests of the target group within the larger culture (*psychographics*.) What are their interests? What do they value? What are their pain points? You're not actually creating for the client but for their customers.

4. Approach every project not just with getting it done and getting paid, but what you can learn from developing it. For every project you accept, evaluate its success once it's completed and functioning for the client, and also what you gained from developing the work. Always be learning, expanding your knowledge and enhancing your skills. Accept projects that fit within your skill set but also push you to step up your game.

5. Learn to lead your clients. Leaders are not entitled to followers; they earn them. Be someone your client looks to for information, ideas, and insight. Be someone open to considering their ideas as well as your own. Be an attentive listener. Be THE creative partner for your clients.

6. Be reliable. Respond to emails. Return telephone calls. Communicate with your client throughout every step of the project. If you're unable to meet a deadline, let the client know, and talk with them about adjustments. Admit where you're weak (everyone lacks in some area). Don't take on projects you truly can't handle. Hand off tasks you don't do well or don't want to do to reliable, proven sub-contractors.

7. Accept critique. Clients have opinions and will express them. Many don't express negative reactions in a constructive manner. Learn to "let things roll off your back". Instead of taking criticism of your work personally, start asking the client questions: "What is it you don't think is working? Why not?" Put the focus on the design instead of on your feelings. Critique is useful to you and will benefit you. You can't improve easily without it.

8. Cultivate creativity. Start by asking, "What if?" Begin with the obvious answers, but don't stop there. What will change the game? What will disrupt the status quo? Look for those answers when developing your creative solutions. Seek inspiration, but let it suggest new ideas. Don't simply reiterate or create a new version.

9. Avoid mediocrity. Excellence is hard work. Are you really in this to be just good enough? Or do you aim to rise above? Go above and beyond. Don't short-change your client or yourself. Always do your best work. Talent is not expertise. Develop your talent and your skill. Back up both with ethics and character.

10. Manage your reputation. Every day, everything you do either adds to or subtracts from your reputation. Be the person your client wants to work with and will eagerly recommend to others.

As a creative you'll focus on either winning projects or building relationships. For any project, it's your responsibility to build the relationship and create high quality work. The main thing is this: Your approach to projects and clients will make you a sought-after creative, and you will not need to worry so much about competing against others, because you will naturally stand out.

Now that we've addressed how you can be the type of creative your clients prefer to work with, we'll move on to the practicalities of working with them.

INQUIRY AND DISCOVERY CONVERSATIONS

It's helpful to distinguish between the inquiry conversation and the discovery conversation. In my practice I don't take the time required for discovery until I'm in a contracted relationship with the client. **Discovery** is the initial deep dive into the client's circumstances that helps uncover driving motivators and assess their needs. It's a paid-for process and the necessary foundation for developing effective solutions for them.

Inquiry is the initial, first contact discussion to know what the prospective client is seeking. In it you want to glean as much basic information as possible to be able to make a decision about working with them.

I developed a list of inquiry questions that I use to determine if a prospect is a good fit for me and I for them. These questions serve as a guide for both of us to determine whether or not to work together. The questions are somewhat Socratic in nature in that they seek to uncover motives and facts:

- What do you want me to do for you? (Why did you contact me?)
- Have you worked with a creative in the past? How did it go?
- What's the nature of your business? What do you provide?
- How long have you been in business?
- Who are your customers (or clients)?
- What's the reason for the project now? What's going on?
- What do you want to accomplish with this project?
- Do you have a budget allocated for this project? How much?
- How did you hear about me?
- Are you talking with other creatives? Which ones? (This pertains to how they perceive you in relation to other options.)

I describe how I approach creative development and manage projects, and answer whatever questions they have for me. I will pass on a project if the prospective client:

- Has budget that's insufficient for the scope of work.
- Treats the inquiry conversation as if it's a job interview.
- Requires me to undertake an unpaid test project.

- Complains about creatives they've worked with in the past.
- Asks me to work with their in-house creative department or with other freelancers they're working with. This runs contrary to my brand positioning: I don't work under someone else's direction or with a creative team I don't direct.
- Declines to share basic information about their business.
- Requests that I take a specific approach in my creative process.

A real life example of that last point happened a number of years ago when a commercial developer approached me to design his storefront and develop his branding based on *feng shui* principles because his wife insisted on it. But because feng shui practices directly contradict my world view, I declined the project offer.

Don't be afraid to decline a project that doesn't fit well. Don't ignore those red flags. When you take on a project your role is to do your work to the best of your ability, set an example, and make the most of every opportunity. Your responsibility is to solve the client's business problem for them. When a prospect doesn't share your point of view, certainly you can work with them. But accept a project only if they're someone you can serve well without compromising your own beliefs and values. Let them see your good works. Be salt and light. *Whatever you do, work heartily, as for the Lord and not for men...* — Colossians 3:23.

THE ONBOARDING AND CREATIVE DEVELOPMENT PROCESSES

Once the client and I decide it's good to work together, I initiate the working relationship and establish expectations before I start the work. Taking the lead is a crucial positioning move that sets the stage for the entire project. Here is the sequence I follow:

Provide the proposal. It includes the project description, deliverables, time budget, financial budget, estimated expenses, and terms of service (the fine print of a contract.) Depending on the client, the proposal also includes the contract. If not, I send the contract after the propose is accepted— in writing.

Provide the contract and invoice for the down payment if the contract is separate from the proposal. If the contract is part of the proposal, I invoice for the down payment. Note that if the client does not sign and return the contract and remit the down payment, I do not begin working on the project. I don't have a client unless and until we're in a contracted relationship.

Orientation. This is the on-boarding process of communicating how the working relationship is structured, including the role the client will play complementary to yours, the boundaries for communication, business hours, when invoices will be sent and payment expected, policies described, and terms reiterated, so that both you and the client know what to expect.

Discovery and/or strategy conversation are a deep dive into the client's reason for being, their mission, vision, existing brand identity, challenges, and more. This is where I cement my role of strategic creative partner. Photographers and illustrators can take the same approach their clients to determine objectives for the work they create. Discussions of brand persona, tone of voice, story arcs, mission statements, etc. will take place. You brainstorm and bounce ideas.

Through the discovery phase of the project you demonstrate your insights and thought leadership. Discovery leads to the **design brief**, which is the list of business and branding objectives and how you intend to address them.

CREATIVE DEVELOPMENT PROCESS

Research. This is your process of determining what's already out there, what can be used as inspiration and source material for your creative solutions. Along with research you should curate based on the design brief.

Ideation. This is the concept development stage, and can include trial and error — rapid prototyping. From here you select the most worthy ideas and create refined designs or comprehensives (still preliminary work) for the client's review. There can be several revisions/iterations and review stages. Anticipate these in your contract.

For example I usually include two review stages and then the final designs. Additional reviews are extra.

Final designs. The finished designs are converted to the needed file formats and transferred to the client. Working files, layered files, and preliminary sketches are transferred only if they're included in the contracted deliverables. I recommend delivering final work product only after receiving final payment.

After completing the project I send a **thank you** note or email. This can include a request for a testimonial or referral. I often follow up with the client a few months later to ask how things are going. Expressing your appreciation for the project and being able to work with the client lets them know you value them.

CHAPTER THIRTY-NINE

CRITIQUE AND FEEDBACK

Dealing with positive and negative feedback.

When you're a creative serving clients or a *creativepreneur* who's making and selling product your work is going to be evaluated. Your clients and customers are quick to share their opinions, leave online reviews, and tell others about their experiences working with you. Critique and feedback are a fact of life.

While we always hope for positive, edifying feedback from a client, and in my experience most clients will provide that, it's a fact that some will find something to complain about in anything you create. Responding to positive critique is easy, but it's the negative track that can send us reeling and cause us to question ourselves and even become concerned whether we'll be paid for our work.

Dealing graciously with unfavorable feedback — especially if it's accented with *ad hominems* — is one of the most difficult but most valuable professional skills you can develop.

RESPONDING TO FAVORABLE CRITIQUE

When your client compliments your ideas and creative effort, you can acknowledge it in a number of ways:

Thank them for their kind words. "Thank you. I appreciate it. I'm glad to know the work hit the target for you."

Reinforce the collaborative nature of your working relationship. "Your confidence in your mission and vision were great starting points for me to develop this logo for you."

Open the door to future work from the client. "You were great to work with. I look forward to tackling future projects together."

Ask for a testimonial to use in your marketing. "May I share your comments on my website?"

RESPONDING TO UNFAVORABLE CRITIQUE

It's crucial to remain professional when critique is negative. Don't take it personally. Even if the client tosses a few character attacks (ad hominems) in your direction, don't take the bait. This is a framework you can use to respond thoughtfully and protect both your professionalism and your creative integrity.

First, **pause.** Let the negative words sit for a moment or two, and even overnight or over the weekend, depending on the situation. Time gives you margin to carefully consider how you respond so that you don't exacerbate their ire.

Second, **acknowledge their feedback**. "I appreciate you sharing your thoughts and impressions."

Respond with Socratic-style questions that dig deeper for motivations and purpose. "Please share what is falling short in the design." Ask for specifics. Is it color? Is it style? Is it typography?

Although there should be a design brief that you and the client agreed on, it can happen that the client will respond based on their personal preferences and not based on the design brief. You have to discern this, and direct them back to the assignment brief, and even your contract. If their reasoning is on the order of, "I don't like the color blue," or "I don't like the way the face is drawn," or "It reminds me of...," recognize that these are expressions of personal opinion and should be addressed in a professional manner by reminding them of the purpose of the work, their audience, what they desire to accomplish with it, and how your creative decisions work to that end. But if the client states that the work doesn't represent their brand well, then you need to determine the ways in which the work misses the mark. In that case, confirm their concerns and discuss options, and offer a new due date to review the revised work.

By referring back to the creative brief and how you addressed the criteria, the client is likely to realize their reaction was subjective and approve the work without modification.

It has happened that a client's critique is disrespectful and their focus is you and not the work. In that case remain calm. This protects your boundaries without escalating emotions. Again, pausing before responding is a useful tactic and demonstrates emotional intelligence. If you respond to the client with high energy or emotion, you'll likely lose the client. Go back over the creative brief and business objectives with the client and explain how your work fulfills them.

Once the client's concerns are resolved, do some reflection. Was their unfavorable feedback warranted? Are there gaps in your skills or communication that you need to address? Were you thorough in developing the creative brief? Did you listen well to the client's objectives?

Keep in mind that it's important to reference the brief any time you present preliminary work and final designs. This reminds the client of the agreed-upon objectives and gives you the basis for your creative decisions. No matter what your area of expertise — photography, illustration, design — keep the brief close at hand and refer to it often to stay on target.

CHAPTER FORTY

HUMANITY AND TECHNOLOGY

Freelancing in the age of artificial intelligence

Technological advances have always caused concern and subsequent adjustment in the creative professions. Case in point was the transition that took place in the late 1980s when we shifted from paste-up and the use of pica poles to digital mediums. CAD software replaced manual drafting. By 1994 design and graphic production on the computer were standardized in the creative professions, eliminating the need for copy-fitting, stat cameras, typesetting services, and process cameras. During the 1990s the graphic arts professions grew more than 300% as new roles were necessitated and fueled by tech. Architecture professions were impacted by BIM and 3D modeling. Digital photography replaced darkroom processes, while digital video and audio restructured the film and music industries. Augmented reality (AR) and virtual reality (VR) expanded the capabilities of graphic, game, and web designers, enabling creatives and their clients to experience immersive environments. Artificial intelligence and machine learning brought easy automation to creative workflows. Cloud-based collaboration, virtual conferencing and wi-fi enabled the expansion of global market regions. Creatives can now live anywhere, including as nomads, and serve clients internationally with ease. And generative AI is shifting the creation of design solutions from sketching out concepts to writing detailed prompts and using algorithms.

Technology always creates both challenges and opportunities. The independent creative needs to not only keep up but know how to incorporate it into their processes and systems.

OPPORTUNITIES OF AI

Improved efficiency and productivity is one way that artificial intelligence can help you grow your freelance business. AI helps you systematize business and creative tasks including research, ideation, social media posting, drafting copy, scheduling, invoicing, video and image editing, and project and promotion tracking.

The ideation process is accelerated with the use of text prompts in generative AI, allowing you to get to viable solutions quickly.

Content generation for marketing and thought leadership is a key opportunity that can help you overcome creative block.

Creatives can quickly generate and edit images. AI has become a standardized tool within design and imaging software.

CHALLENGES OF AI

Because AI is a learning model (LM) and, as of this writing, does not use critical thinking to differentiate between and among the content it scrapes, it's actually stupid in many ways. While it can cross-reference it can't compare and contrast. It takes directly from what already exists, so it's not a creative tool. Originality, intellectual property, and bias in AI-generated content bring ethical concerns in a number of industries. Copyright for intellectual property generated by AI tools cannot be registered because it lacks human input and control.

It's obvious that we humans will need to continually learn and adapt to changing AI tools and workflows, and also remain cautious about the reliability of information they generate.

Direct impact on you as a freelance creative is that you'll need to carefully manage your client expectations in regard to your use of AI and also whether your work is truly original or generated. Why would a client pay you a high value creative fee if they can generate what they need instantly at a fraction of your price?

You also will find yourself needing to quickly shift your focus, processes, and markets. Positioning and differentiation of your brand is increasingly complex because you're not simply competing for work against other creatives and their brands, but against simulated human intelligence tools.

AI AND YOUR CLIENTS

Creatives are integrating AI tools into their workflows to accelerate prototyping and iteration and automate repetitive tasks. AI is used for creating mood boards, custom assets, and personalized designs. AI is meant to enhance rather than replace human creativity, but we can become lazy by using it as a shortcut to necessary problem-solving activities.

Should you disclose your use of AI in your creative processes to your clients? That depends on how much of your work is directly AI-generated. If you are in the logo design business and rely on AI to generate basic ideas that you then modify, tweak and alter to a great degree, you may not need to disclose your use, just as you don't need to explain what software you use, or that you do your best work at 3:00 AM. But if you use AI in a significant way and your clients expect bespoke, custom, human-created solutions, you should disclose your use of AI and for what purpose. Why should a client pay creative fees for bespoke solutions created by an expert human being if you're providing AI-generated graphics or images that are minimally altered? This is a matter of ethics, integrity, and authenticity. Your clients need to use your work product for their business growth without being hindered.

COPYRIGHT PROTECTION AND AI

Freelance creatives develop and sell products of thought and creative problem-solving — intellectual property. Copyright laws protect human creators from theft and misuse of their work, and protect their ability to profit from what they create.

Copyright protects works created by human beings. A graphic that's entirely AI-generated cannot be legally registered and cannot be claimed for copyright. For works that are both human and AI generated, only the human-created component is protected and can be registered. The copyright registration application must disclose any appreciable AI-generated content in the work. Using AI to sharpen an image or change a color is not appreciable and doesn't need to be disclosed.

PROTECTING YOUR WORK FROM IP THEFT

Because AI is a learning model it sends feelers out into the digital space to seek and capture data and information, including what's on your website and social platforms. The problem of protecting your work from intellectual property (IP) theft is not new, but AI has exacerbated the problem. The likelihood of your work being stolen by nefarious characters impacts not just you as a creative but your clients as well. These are some ways to reduce the likelihood of IP theft of your work:

Embed metadata into your images. Metadata includes the creator's name, date of creation, title of the work, file type, keywords, copyright notice, and other identifying information.

Embed your metadata to link the Google Licensable Image Badge. Google's "Licensable" badge on image search results reveals that an image includes licensing information and allows others to find and potentially license the image for their use. To find licensable images, users can filter their image searches by usage rights such as Creative Commons or commercial use. If you do not want to or cannot offer an image for license, do not include triggering metadata in the image.

Include a copyright notice in your website footer and terms of service text.

Register your copyrights with the United States Copyright Office. You already own the copyright to what you create, but registration gives you the basis to take legal action. You won't register the work you create for clients, generally, but what you create for your branding and marketing, as well as certain products you might sell, should be registered.

Include an AI restriction clause on your website terms of service page. This will give you some leverage should your copyright be infringed and you decide to take legal action.

Add a ghosted watermark on your images. If you set the watermark to 10% or less opacity the watermark will be barely visible but still very present.

If you're an illustrator, include your **signature with a copyright notice** and the date of creation in addition to your watermark. Photographers, designers, and illustrators can include a **visible copyright notice** along the edge of an image.

Become familiar with and support the **DMCA** (Digital Millennium Copyright Act) which updated US copyright law in 1998 to include online content. The DMCA enhances the ability of creators to protect their digital work, and provides for takedown actions when you find your work' has been used without your permission. There are certain procedures you need to follow when requesting a takedown.

While nothing is 100% effective against IP theft, by implementing these options you can reduce the likelihood that your work will be stolen. Also, be aware of how and where you're sourcing images. Do everything you can to avoid infringing someone else's copyright. Treat others the way you want to be treated. — LUKE 6:31

EMBRACING AI AND KEEPING IT HUMAN

The work we create are products of thought and problem-solving. Human-created IP solutions are eligible for legal protection through copyright registration, whereas AI-generated work is not. Therefore you should protect your copyright, incorporate copyright transfer clauses into your contract terms, and be circumspect about how you yourself utilize AI in your creative development processes and business systems.

AI imitates but can't innovate. Innovation is a human-only trait. When it comes to positioning, differentiating, and marketing your creativity, **keep it human.** Capitalize on the fact that you're a human being serving fellow human beings. Innovation and creativity must become inherent not only in your work product but in how you build your business. Emphasize your human capital in marketing and business systems. Foster connections using your unique voice, origin story, and approach. Use case studies describing how you solved a client's problem, and share their testimonials. Invite your audience to connect and communicate with you human-to-human.

Build a thoughtfully crafted brand. Your influence and reputation are unique and cannot be mimicked by AI. Branding isn't about visual assets and elevator pitches. Its job is to establish emotional responses, connect your audience to you, and engender loyalty by leveraging your humanity. A strategically-crafted brand functions as a signal in a landscape of AI-generated attempts at creativity. Your personal and professional brand is a unique identity that AI cannot duplicate. So focus on your humanity.

In summary, AI is changing the landscape for all creatives. As with any tool, we can seize it as opportunity instead of threat. Our ability to solve problems for our clients lies not only in our talents and capabilities, but also in our ability to observe, listen, discern, understand, innovate, iterate, think, and create. We're enabled through our divine callings to rise to the challenges presented to us and prevail, press through, and accomplish our purposes.

CHAPTER FORTY-ONE

PURSUING YOUR DREAMS

You're in it for the long haul.

"How do I know if I will be successful at freelancing?" I asked this very question of my teachers when I was in design school, and have been asked by the people I teach. My answer is the same as what my teachers gave me: "You don't know."

No one knows if they will succeed or not. But one thing everyone does know is that you will not succeed if you do not go after it. Waiting until you know you will succeed to start your freelance career, to pursue that one big project, to add a new service, or to reinvent yourself, is wasted time. Get moving, or nothing will happen.

It takes more than talent and desire to be successful at anything. Both are necessary, but how many talented people don't make much of their God-given gifts because they don't start and keep moving?

Neither talent nor fear will motivate. We have to decide to do something and then do it. Here are five things you can do to help create your success:

1. **Set specific, achievable goals.** Goals give you direction and are the stepping stones leading to your success. You cannot be successful at something until you first decide what that something is and then plan how you will get there. Write down your goals, list the steps you need to take to achieve them, and keep this document close at hand. Track and review your progress regularly.

Your goals should encompass your whole life, not only your business. They should address your creative work and your business, as well as the family, household, physical, and spiritual aspects of your life and being. If you're a believer, commit your goals to God according to the admonition in Proverbs 37:5 NKJV: *Commit your way to the LORD, Trust also in Him, And He shall bring it to pass.*

2. **Work on your goals.** Writing them down is only a first step. The next step is to move forward on them task-by-task and action-by-action. Schedule time every day for goal-related actions, and then follow through. Daily effort means you are consistently building momentum. Sacrificing distractions and certain activities

I spend the first hour of my days in Bible reading, study, journaling and planning my agenda. I look at my larger goals at the end of each week, identify my next steps that will move me forward, and add them to my schedule for the upcoming week. Once a month I spend at least half a day reviewing, assessing, correcting, and setting new goals with a one to three year overview.

3. **Learn from people** who are successful at doing what you want to do. What do they offer to the world? How does it benefit their customers and clients? How do they promote their work? What is the quality of their work? Do some investigating by looking at web sites reading blogs, and watching videos, observing and critiquing their work and the results of their work. Take notes. Engage in networking, take classes, attend seminars and webinars. There is wisdom in a multitude of counselors.

4. **Ask someone to hold you accountable.** This someone can be a trusted family member, friend, colleague, or mentor. It can be a mastermind group or a business coach. It can be in person or virtually, or both. Share your goals with them and allow them to check in with you at regular intervals — once a month, once a quarter, for example — heed their feedback and allow them to encourage you. The point is that you'll go farther faster with help from others than you will if you're running solo.

5. **Enjoy each small step and victory**. I've learned that simply making one small decision and completing one small step can be enough of an achievement to propel myself forward to do the next thing. Success is a journey — like a road trip. It's accomplished through a series of small steps all going in a particular direction. Along the way, you will pass milestones. When you pass a milestone — complete a project or achieve a goal — celebrate it.

ADJUST WHEN NECESSARY

Becoming successful is not a straight road. There are curves and obstacles to navigate. I have had to adjust my route many times during my freelance career. Some of those adjustments were due to taking wrong turns, some due to new construction, and some due to running out of fuel. I made corrections, re-routed, and kept going. **Once you start moving toward success, knowing if you will succeed or not becomes less of an unknown.** The farther along the road you go — the more progress you make — the nearer you get to your destination, and the more likely you are to succeed.

Wherever you are right now in your freelance career, whether thinking about it, starting out, or in the middle of it, I encourage you to take the next step and continue to move forward.

APPENDICES

APPENDIX A

A FREELANCE ROAD MAP

This road map is a fairly comprehensive, start to finish road map for launching and growing your independent creative business. It expands on what I cover in this book. How might you use this? Think of it in terms of a checklist for what to consider as you plan, launch, and build your freelance business. I've attempted to put them in sequential order within each category. These are building blocks on which you establish your foundation, develop the structure and systems necessary to reach your desired destination, and avoid and bust through common challenges and roadblocks.

MINDSET

- Your role as a creative
- Your role as a business owner
- Value of your skills, talents, gifts
- Your philosophy and world view
- Introvert or extrovert
- Your working style
- Risk awareness & avoidance
- Your internal motivators
- Owner vs. employee differentiation
- Hobbyist or professional creative
- Part-time or full-time
- Lifestyle
  - Stationary
  - Nomadic
- Health & creative energy cycles
- Work-life integration

MISSION

- Your purpose/divine calling
- Your vision and mission
- Your expertise
- Goals and objectives
- SWOT analysis
- Your competitive advantage
- Your unique selling proposition (USP)
- Your learning and education
- How you solve business problems
- Services you offer
- Thought leadership

MECHANICS

- Your workspace & equipment
- Internet & connectivity
- Funding, banking, credit
- Insurance
- Business plan
- Pricing
  - Time-based
  - Value-based
  - Fee Schedule
  - Retainer
  - Negotiating
    - Price, cost, and value
    - Anchoring
- Budget & accounting
- Income/Expenses, profit & loss
- Licenses & permits
- Business entity (LLC, S-corp, proprietor)
- Recordkeeping

MECHANICS continued

- Business policies
- Business systems & automation
- Contracts, proposals, invoices
- Project tracking
- Scheduling & time management
  - Time blocking
  - Task batching
- Policy & advocacy
- Income diversification
  - Recurring revenue
  - Passive income
- Online store
- Growth & scaling
- Internal Struggles
- External Struggles
- Client relations
  - Ideal client profile
  - Business problems to solve
  - Communication
  - Onboarding
  - Managing expectations
  - Retention

MESSAGING & MARKETING

- Brand, personal and professional
- Marketing strategy, tactics, plan
- List building
- Testimonials & reviews
- Networking groups & service clubs
- Marketing tools
  - Website/blog
  - Social media
  - Email/newsletters
- Video/podcast
- Search engines
  - Optimization
  - Indexing
  - Key words and phrases, search terms
- Offline media (print, direct mail)
- Press releases
- Contests
- Business listings & creative directories

SUCCESS METRICS

- Customer Lifetime Value (CLV)
- Retention Rate
- Key performance indicators
- Cost per lead
- Profit margin
- Repeat business rate
- Net referral scores
- Project value vs. duration

APPENDIX B

FREELANCE CONTRACT TERMS

Contracts are a necessary part of doing business. They help manage expectations in the working relationship between freelance creative and client, and help prevent misunderstandings. They protect both parties. Structure your own contracts to best represent your own interests, and learn to read and assess contracts offered by clients. The following clauses are examples of what I include in my contract terms of service. You're free to use and modify these clauses to fit your needs.

The Agreement for the Project described in the Scope of Work to which these terms and conditions are attached (the "Project") shall consist of the final Scope of Work. Fees and Costs Estimate, and Timeline, these terms and conditions, and any change orders set forth in writing and executed by the Designer and the Client subsequent to the acceptance of the original Scope of Work. Changes to the Scope of Work may result in adjustments to the charges and the production schedule for the Project.

The performance of the strategy, design and production services, and delivery of tangible and/or intellectual property described in this proposal/contract (the "Agreement") of which these terms and conditions are a part, is governed by the following terms and conditions. Unless otherwise agreed in writing, [insert your name or business name here] expressly rejects any additional or different terms or conditions proposed by the Client.

PAYMENTS: Payment for creative services will be made as follows. One third of the Estimated Design and Production Fees ($ <u>insert specific amount here</u>) is due upon acceptance of the proposal. Payment may be made by check or credit card. The deposit is non-refundable. Subsequent invoices will be submitted every 14 days for the duration of the project, currently estimated at 6 weeks. The final invoice will include any and all expenses for vendors, service providers, specialists or subcontractors engaged in accordance with the proposal Expenses not paid in advance by the Client) will be due upon final approval of the Project. Except for the portions of invoices that are disputed in good faith by the Client for not being in accordance with the terms and conditions of this Agreement, any amounts not paid when due shall accrue interest at the rate of 1.5% per month from the date due until paid. The Designer reserves the right to withhold delivery of all final electronic and/or printed materials and files until the undisputed portion(s) of overdue invoices are paid. Client assumes responsibility for all collection and legal fees necessitated by default in payment.

EXPENSES: Client shall reimburse Designer for all expenses arising from this assignment, including the payment of any sales taxes due on this assignment, and shall advance $0 to the Designer for payment of said expenses. Expenses are estimated, and approved by Client prior to outlay. All outside expenses, including but not limited to: Photography, Illustration, Copy writing, Printing, Fonts, Images, Licenses, and Color Outputs will be billed with a surcharge of 20% of vendor costs. The surcharge will not be applied to Deliveries and Postage.

CHANGES: Revisions or author's alterations to the Scope of Work shall obligate the Client to additional fees and costs. These may include but are not limited to: changes made to copy after the final copy has been submitted; changes made to the design once layouts, website design, or site map have been approved; extensive alterations; a change in marketing objectives on the part of the Client, and new work requested by the Client after the execution of this Agreement. All production costs are based on the assumption that copy will be provided electronically. Change orders will be prepared by the Designer and provided to the Client outlining the changes to the Scope of Work, and any additional costs and schedule impact for those changes. The Client agrees to pay the Designer additional fees and costs for said revisions or alterations at a rate of $175.00 per hour. Hourly rates quoted in proposals will remain in effect until further written notice is given. If the Designer is unable to meet the delivery schedule set forth in the Agreement due to delays by Client or changes requested by Client in the Scope of Work, the Designer may, in her/his discretion, revise the production schedule as necessary and provide for adjustments in the costs for the Project.

IMMEDIACY/OVERTIME: Estimates are based on normal and reasonable time schedules, and may have to be revised to take into consideration any "rush" requests requiring overtime or weekends. Knowledge of the Client's deadlines is essential to provide an accurate estimate of costs. The Designer's overtime incurred at the Client's request will be billed at a rate of $175.00 per hour. The Client will also be responsible for additional charges imposed by outside suppliers, such as retouchers or printers, to meet Client's "rush" requests.

To the extent possible, the Designer will advise Client of all situations that require overtime and/or rush charges, and the amount of additional compensation that will be charged to meet such overtime requirements or rush requests. Rush or overtime fees may be incurred if the Client does not meet approval or content deadlines which have been established to meet the Client's desired schedule.

OWNERSHIP AND USAGE RIGHTS: The rights to be granted by the Designer under this Agreement will be transferred to the Client once full payment for services and expenses is made by Client to the Designer. Upon receipt of full payment, the Client is hereby granted "All Rights" which are exclusive and unlimited usage and reproduction rights to the final designs prepared for Client as part of this Project. Except for the foregoing license, all right, title and interest to all designs and artwork (whether draft or final versions, whether digital or hard copy) remain with the Designer or her contractors or vendors, as applicable. This includes, but is not limited to, layouts, animations and designs created by the Designer or her contractors or vendors, computer drives containing such layouts, photography, or illustration created by independent photographers or illustrators commissioned by the Designer, and photography or other images purchased by the Designer from a stock agency on the Client's behalf. The Designer reserves the right to reproduce any and all designs created by the Designer in print and electronic media for her promotional purposes for an unlimited period of time. The Designer has the right to retain, or if applicable, Client agrees to provide the Designer with, five (5) printed samples of each tangible product produced as a result of the Project. In developing any brand marks, the Designer will use reasonable commercial efforts, consistent with standards in the industry, to ensure that any such brand marks are original.

ORIGINALITY The Designer's efforts shall not include a complete trademark clearance search. Should a higher level of assurance be required by Client, the services of a trademark search firm and intellectual property attorney should be retained by Client.

NON-DISCLOSURE OF CONFIDENTIAL INFORMATION Neither Party will, at any time, whether during or after the termination or expiration of this Agreement, for any reason whatsoever, disclose to any person or entity or use for any purpose other than fulfilling its obligations hereunder, the other Party's Confidential Information, as defined in the existing NDA. Any concepts, business strategies, trademarks, service marks, materials, outlines, etc., provided to one Party by the other Party constitute trade secrets and Confidential Information under this Agreement and shall not be used by the other Party for any other purpose than for the purpose of the Project.

CONFIDENTIAL INFORMATION Confidential Information means all confidential and proprietary information of either Party, including, without limitation, information relating to: the business; trade secret information; client, investor, customer and supplier lists, and contracts or arrangements; financial information; market research and development procedures, processes, techniques, plans and results; investment or acquisition opportunities, pricing information or policies; computer software, passwords, programs or data; and all other business related information, whether such information is in written, graphic, recorded, electronic, photographic, data or any machine readable form or is orally conveyed to or developed by the other Party; provided that Confidential Information shall not include information which: (a) is in or hereafter enters the public domain through no fault of the receiving party; (b) is obtained by the receiving party from a third party having the legal right to use and disclose the same; (c) is in the possession of the receiving party prior to receipt from the disclosing party, as evidenced by the receiving party's written records pre-dating such receipt; (d) is independently developed by the receiving party as evidenced by written record proving such independence; or, (e) is required to be disclosed by governmental order or judicial subpoena, provided that prior to disclosure the receiving party shall give the disclosing party prior notice to allow the disclosing party an opportunity to obtain an appropriate protective order.

RETURN OF CONFIDENTIAL INFORMATION Each Party shall, upon the request of the other Party, return to the other Party all written or other descriptive materials containing Confidential Information or otherwise relating to the other Party, its business and its intellectual property, including, but not limited to, drawings, blueprints, descriptions, notes, analyses or other papers or documents which contain any such information. In any event, upon the completion or expiration of this Agreement, or if this Agreement is terminated for any reason, each Party shall, without request by the other party, return all aforementioned Confidential Information; provided that each party may retain one archival copy of the Confidential Information, solely for the purpose of determining its obligations under this Agreement.

INDEMNIFICATION Each Party shall indemnify, defend, and hold harmless the other and its affiliates, officers, agents, and employees, from any and all claims, suits, actions, demands, damages, liabilities, expenses (including reasonable fees and disbursements of counsel), judgments, settlements and penalties of every kind that may be asserted or incurred including but not limited to: (a) any breach by such Party of any trademark, trade name and/or copyright infringement, invasion of privacy, defamation, or other wrongful use of any pictures, photographs, images, copy or other materials; and/or (b) the negligent, intentionally wrongful or illegal acts or omissions of such Party, its employees, agents, subcontractors or other representatives and/or (c) violations of any federal, state, local and/or international laws, rules and/or regulations to which such Party is subject.

APPLICABLE LAW/DISPUTE RESOLUTION This agreement shall be governed by, and construed under, the laws of the State of California. In the event of a dispute arising under this Agreement, the dispute shall be finally settled by arbitration under the Rules of the American Arbitration Association (the "AAA"). The Arbitration shall be held in Thousand Oaks, CA. The arbitration shall be held before a single arbitrator, selected in accordance with the rules of the AAA. The arbitrator's award shall be final and shall be enforceable in any court of competent jurisdiction. The arbitrator shall award the prevailing party its costs of such arbitration including, but not limited to, reasonable attorneys' fees. If a party refuses to comply with the rendered award, and the other party enters an application for judicial enforcement thereof, the refusing party shall bear all of the expenses incurred in connection with such application. Nothing in this paragraph shall prevent either party from resorting to judicial process if injunctive or other equitable relief from a court is necessary to prevent serious and irreparable injury to one party or to others.

CANCELLATION: In the event the Client cancels this Agreement prior to the completion of the Project, ownership of all copyrights for original artwork, and ownership of sketches, notes, refinements, whether on paper or digital, created for this Project shall be retained by the Designer. Within five (5) business days of such cancellation, the Client shall pay (a) the Designer for all work performed by the Designer up to the date of termination, if the work has not been pre-paid, (b) for all contracted for Outside Expenses and commitments that have been incurred and cannot be cancelled and [c] a cancellation fee equal to 15% of the remaining fees that would otherwise have been paid to the Designer if the Agreement were to have been fully performed.

ERRORS The Client has the responsibility to proofread and examine all work produced during the Project. Therefore, the Client is ultimately responsible for any typographical, spelling, grammatical, copy, photographic, illustrative, layout, content accuracies or omissions, or other errors discovered after printing, deployment, or reproduction, or for any work or services performed by any party selected by the Client. In the event the Client determines that there are errors in the work produced during the Project, Client shall notify the Designer of any errors within 48 hours of Client's determination. Failure to promptly notify The Designer shall constitute a waiver by Client of any claim arising out of such errors.

PERFORMANCE Each party shall use commercially reasonable efforts or fulfill its obligations hereunder, but shall in no event be responsible for any failure or delay in performance due to any catastrophe, act of God or government authority, civil strife, or any other cause beyond the control of such party. In no event shall the Designer's liability exceed the sum of payments received from the Client under this Agreement. Neither party shall be liable to the other for any consequential, indirect, special or punitive damages, even if such damage were reasonably foreseeable.

PRICING The prices set forth in this Agreement are valid through [date], and represent the Designer's good-faith estimate of costs included in the price. If printing is a component of this estimate, printing prices are not guaranteed until printing has been ordered. The designer shall inform Client promptly if any variations in costs or outside expenses are anticipated.

WAIVER Any waiver by either party, whether express or implied, of any provision of this Agreement, any waiver of default, or any course of dealing hereunder, shall not affect such party's right to thereafter enforce such provision or to exercise any right or remedy in the event of any other default or breach whether or not similar.

SEVERABILITY If any provision of this Agreement shall be deemed void in whole or in part for any reason whatsoever, the remaining provisions shall remain in full force and effect.

INDEPENDENT CONTRACTOR In performing their respective obligations under this Agreement, the parties agree that their relationship is that of independent contractors and not that of a partners, joint venturers, agents, employees or part-time employees of the other party. Neither party will represent itself as, act or purport to act as or be deemed to be the agent, representative, employee or servant of the other party.

CONTROL: The Designer is the sole determiner of when, how, and where work is performed, and is not available for communication (email, text message, or telephone) or conferences outside of regular business hours.

NOTICES If either party is required or permitted to send the other party any notices, such notices shall be in writing and sent to the other party at its last business address or their registered agent, by registered or certified mail, postage prepaid, return receipt requested or by private overnight delivery service, return receipt requested. Notices shall be effective upon receipt.

ENTIRE AGREEMENT This Agreement and the attachments hereto represent the entire agreement between The Designer with respect to the performance of the Creative Services and supersedes any prior oral or written agreements of discussions, may not be modified or amended unless in writing signed by each of the parties, and may not be assigned by either party without the written consent of the other party which consent will not be unreasonably withheld.

APPENDIX C

SUPPORT FOR FREELANCERS

A curated list of professional and business resources for freelance creatives resides online at:
freelanceroadtrip.com/resources-for-creative-freelancers/

Join the Freelance Road Trip email list:
freelanceroadtrip.com/newsletter

Get access to the Freelance Road Trip Business School courses:
freelanceroadtrip.com

APPENDIX D

GLOSSARY OF BUSINESS TERMS

When working with businesses and organizations it's appropriate to speak their language. To help you speak confidently when doing business I compiled this list of commonly used business terms and definitions that can help you communicate and build trust with your clients.

Accounts Receivable
Money owed, but not yet collected, by customers to a business for goods and services sold by the business. Amounts your customers owe you but haven't yet paid. *Example: You complete a project and invoice the client. Until they pay you, the sum they owe you is considered an accounts receivable.* Similarly, **accounts payable** is the money you owe to others but have not yet paid.

Assets
Anything of economic value that an individual or enterprise owns. Equipment, real estate, inventory, stocks, cash, crypto, and artwork are all assets and are factored into one's net worth.

Blue Ocean Strategy
A strategic approach focused on creating uncontested market space by differentiating from existing competitors in products, services, and/or marketing.

Brand
The unique identity of a product, service, or company. A business's or person's reputation and known-fors.

Business-to-Business (B2B)
Commerce transactions between businesses. Selling to other businesses rather than consumers or the government. *Example: Most of the time you, as a freelancer, work with businesses or non-profits, not with consumers. Your clients may also be B2B enterprises.*

Business-to-Consumer (B2C)
The sale of goods and services from businesses to the end-user. Selling to people, as in retail. Examples: You diversify your income sources by developing and selling a line of greeting cards based on your illustrations.

Business Model
A framework outlining how a company creates, delivers, and captures value for its customers.

Business Plan
A formal proposal outlining business goals, the reasons for them, the desired outcomes and the steps to reach those goals. Business plans are often used to acquire funding, but are vital in any case for setting clear goals and priorities to become successful.

Cash Flow
A revenue or expense stream that changes a cash account of a given period of time. The difference between how LONG it takes your clients to pay you relative to how LITTLE time you have to pay your bills. Example: A client takes 30 days to pay your invoice but your mortgage is due in 10 days. If you don't have enough cash on hand to cover the mortgage while you wait for client payment, you will be out of business quickly. Negative cash flow often results in accumulating more debt, and has killed countless freelance businesses.

Competitive Advantage
A definable factor that gives a company an edge over its competitors in the market.

Core Competency
A specialized skill or capability that sets a company apart from competitors and contributes significantly to its competitive advantage.

Cushion
Reserve funds. Money left after a company has met its payment obligations and is set aside to meet unexpected needs. Cushion can be taken from profit to create an emergency fund or set aside to pay taxes rather than relying on credit cards and running up debt to do so.

Customer Lifetime Value (CLV)
The cumulative revenue from a client or customer over a set time period. It's the amount of money a client will spend on your services for the duration of their time working with you. We use CLV to determine what types of clients to work with, and whether to focus on client acquisition or retention. For example: I've worked with one client on a recurring annual project for close to two decades, and I've netted close to $150,000 from that client alone.

Customer Relationship Management (CRM)
A software or manual system that helps businesses manage interactions with customers and prospects.

Data Analytics
The process of examining, transforming, and cleansing data to identify useful information, inform conclusions, and support decision-making.

Double-Entry Bookkeeping
A system of bookkeeping that records every financial transaction twice, once in a debit account and once in a credit account.

Entrepreneurship
The process of starting a business and taking on the risks associated with it.

First To Market (First Mover) Advantage
The benefit gained by being the first to launch a service or product in a market. This can result in strong brand awareness, customer loyalty, and the ability to acquire key resources before competitors enter the market.

Gross and Net
Gross is the total amount before any deductions or expenses. Net is the amount remaining after all deductions and expenses have been subtracted. *For example, you bill your client $2,586.10 for a project, including expenses and sales taxes totaling $386.10. The client pays with a credit card, and your processing fee for the transaction is $77.58. Your net income for that invoice is $2,122.42.* There's often a question of whether to tithe on one's gross (first fruits) or net income (increase). Tithing is a choice, and how you tithe is also your choice. Paul provides a guiding principle in 2 Corinthians 9:7: "Each one should give what he has decided in his heart to give, not out of regret or compulsion. For God loves a cheerful giver." He also observed in 2 Corinthians 8:12: "If the willingness is there, the gift is acceptable according to what one has, not according to what one does not have." In any case, it's unwise to tithe yourself into a negative cash flow. No matter whether you give based on your gross or your net, your motive should be a reverent, grateful response to God's provision given out of your own free will and not out of obligation.

Intellectual Property (IP)
Intangible, protectable creations of the human mind, including inventions, literary and artistic works, designs, and symbols.

Invoice
A document issued by a seller to the buyer, showing the agreed prices for products or services the seller has provided to the buyer. *Example: You send invoices to your clients asking them to pay what they owe to you. Your vendors send you invoices asking you to pay them.*

Key Performance Indicator (KPI)
A metric or measurement used to define whether an you're meeting a predefined goal. They're necessary indicators of the progress you're making toward your business objectives. *For example, I set the goal of writing and publishing this book. My indicators were to have specific actions accomplished by certain calendar dates, and I'd have the book written and published in 12 months. When I didn't meet my deadline I had to take a serious look at why (mainly due to distractions) and then reset my goals and adjust my performance. You're reading the result, but it's been a few years getting this goal done. If you don't measure, you won't get things done. When you set a goal, it should be measured and scheduled or you won't do it.*

Liabilities
Anything that's owed to another. Student and other types of loan debt, credit card debt, leases, income taxes and other tax obligations, and amounts you owe to your vendors are liabilities.

Marketing Mix
The four key elements of a marketing strategy: product, price, placement, and promotion.

Minimum Viable Product (MVP)
A version of a product or service that has just enough features and benefits for the customer or client to be usable, with the intention of improving it after it's launched. It's the simplest product or service that's still marketable. *For example, you might launch your freelance design business creating logos and graphics for fellow members of your gaming community, with the intention of working with small businesses within 12 months.*

Negotiation
The process of discussing and reaching agreement on a common course of action, often involving compromise.

Non-Disclosure Agreement (NDA)
A legal contract that protects confidential information disclosed by one party to another.

Opportunity Cost
The cost of something not pursued that must be forgone in order to pursue a different action. It's the cost of what you give up in order to do something else.
Example: You are considering enrolling the Freelance Road Trip Business School to be able to gain necessary business skills and insights to increase your future profitability. If you don't enroll, the opportunity cost is the future profit increase. If you do enroll, the opportunity cost is the time spent on the coursework that could be applied to getting new projects. Given the choice between two or more alternatives, there's always an opportunity cost.

Overhead/Operating Expense
The ongoing expenses of operating a business. What it costs to operate your business regardless of whether or not you have clients. Example: Insurance, office supplies, software subscriptions, utilities, advertising, taxes, and anything else that's required to stay in business but doesn't directly generate revenue.

Production Capacity
The volume of services you can provide utilizing current resources. How much work you can produce. There is a finite amount of work each of us can do, a finite amount of time, and therefore a finite amount of money we can earn. Task batching, time blocking, and automating your business can free up time and save creative energy. Outsourcing and delegating can also increase your production capacity. As an independent creative there are certain types of clients you won't be able to work with unless you outsource or scale your business into an agency. *For example, a number of years ago I considered advertising on a local radio talk show. I was dissuaded by the station's marketing rep because they weren't convinced I was equipped to handle the amount of work that would result. Wanting to remain a consultancy, I chose not to advertise.*

Profit
The difference between an enterprise's total revenue and its costs – how much money you have left over after you've paid all of your expenses. Profit is not revenue. Example: You invoice a client $1,200 for a brochure that costs you $700 to produce. Your profit on that project is $500.

Profit Margin
Revenue - Cost/Revenue * 100. A ratio of profitability calculated by finding the net profit as a percentage of revenue. The percentage of how much profit you make. *Example: You photograph 15 products for your client's e-commerce website at the flat rate of $1500. It costs you $1,000 in time to shoot, edit, and format the images. Your profit margin for the project is 33%: $1,500 - $1,000/$1,500 * 100. When you calculate your profit margins on projects you learn which clients create more profit and which create less and make adjustments that result in higher profit margins.*

Return on Investment (ROI)
The efficiency of an investment, or the comparison of efficiencies of a number of different investments. *Example: You invest 120 hours developing digital brand assets for a client at a value-based rate of $10K. If your hourly is set at $65.00, you've invested $7,800 of your time, with no expenses, giving you a return of $2,200 on your investment.*

Search Engine Optimization (SEO)
The practice of improving the ranking of a website on search engine results pages (SERPs) to increase organic traffic. Boost SEO through keywords and key phrases, backlinks, and most importantly, quality content.

SWOT Analysis
A strategic planning framework that helps businesses evaluate their Strengths, Weaknesses, Opportunities, and Threats. Strengths and weaknesses are internal assessments, while opportunities and threats are external.

Unique Selling Proposition (USP)
A distinct advantage that sets a company's product or service apart from competitors.

Value Proposition
A concise statement that explains the specific benefits customers receive from a business's product or service, highlighting how the offering solves the customer's problem or fulfills their needs.

Vendor (Supplier)
A person or business that sells to your business. A business or individual who supplies goods or services to you so you can do business. *Example: You buy art supplies from Blick, web hosting from Siteground, and payment processing from Stripe. These are vendors.*

Acknowledgements

My thanks to and appreciation for these highly-valued people who have encouraged me in the creation of this book:

Deanna Byford
Michelle Katz
Lynn Lee
KayLynn Lundgren
Rev. Kenneth Lundgren
Eleanor Schraeder
Sarah Tirzah

SHIFT INTO FREELANCING WITHOUT STALLING OUT

Business School for Freelance Creatives

Free newsletter. Join the mailing list.

Listen to the Freelance Road Trip Podcast

About the Author

For more than four decades, **Alvalyn Lundgren** has been freelancing and teaching. In 1993 she established Alvalyn Creative as a strategic consultancy to help her clients grow their enterprises through brand strategy, visual design, and illustration. Her client roster includes notable brands including Epson, Baxalta US, City of Los Angeles, Southern California Edison, and California State University, Northridge, as well as numerous small and mid-size businesses and organizations. Alongside her design practice she is a respected teacher of creative skills and creative business in design programs with UCLA Extension, ArtCenter College of Design Extended Studies, and independently. Her *Eye Level* blog about design, drawing, and visual perception attracts thousands of readers, and she serves a growing YouTube audience. An advocate of art and design as viable professions, she founded Freelance Road Trip to teach business skills to creatives, sharing what she learned from building her own business so that others can learn from her mistakes and avoid making their own. She is the creator and host of the *Freelance Road Trip* podcast and the Occuprise Network, and is currently developing an online academy to teach aspiring illustrators and designers key skills to practice professionally. Alvalyn resides in Southern California, enjoys road trip adventures, and has journeyed to all fifty US states and eight Canadian provinces by automobile, except for Hawaii, to which she first traveled by air and then by car.

ONLINE
alvalyncreative.com
alvalyn.com
freelanceroadtrip.com
academy.alvalyn.com

CONNECT
LinkedIn: /alvalynlundgren
X: /FreelanceTrip

www.ingramcontent.com/pod-product-compliance
Lightning Source LLC
LaVergne TN
LVHW012047160826
845678LV00014B/2731

9798995300403